Darling, you shouldn't have gone to so much trouble

by Caroline Blackwood

FOR ALL THAT I FOUND THERE
THE STEPDAUGHTER
GREAT GRANNY WEBSTER
(all published by Duckworth)

by Anna Haycraft

THE NATURAL BABYFOOD COOKERY BOOK
(published by Fontana)

as Alice Thomas Ellis

THE SIN EATER
THE BIRDS OF THE AIR
(both published by Duckworth)

Caroline Blackwood
and Anna Haycraft

Darling, you shouldn't have gone to so much trouble

Drawings by Zé

JONATHAN CAPE
THIRTY BEDFORD SQUARE LONDON

First published 1980
Reprinted 1981 (twice)
Text copyright © 1980 by Caroline Blackwood and Anna Haycraft
Illustrations copyright © 1980 by Zé
Jonathan Cape Ltd, 30 Bedford Square, London WC1

British Library Cataloguing in Publication Data

Blackwood, Caroline
Darling, you shouldn't have gone to so much trouble.
1. Cookery
I. Title   II. Haycraft, Anna
641.5   TX717
ISBN 0-224-01834-5

Printed in Great Britain
by W & J Mackay Limited, Chatham

To our daughters

Contents

Acknowledgments	8
Preface	9
First Steps	13
I Ingredients	15
II Gadgets	30
III Measurements	35
IV Presentation and Panache	36
Cocktails	39
First Courses	55
Soups	75
Fish	93
Main Courses	111
Sauces	149
Vegetables and Salads	159
Puddings	177
Coffee	201
Food for Children	205
Index	219

Acknowledgments

We should like to thank the many people who have contributed their recipes and advice, and in particular Charlotte Bielenberg for her invaluable help.

Acknowledgments are due to the *Daily Telegraph* for permission to reproduce Denis Curtis's recipe (p. 123) and *The Cookbook of the Performing Artists of the Kennedy Center* (Washington, 1973), for permission to reproduce Alice Longworth Roosevelt's recipe (p. 199).

Preface

This cookery book is not for beginners. Anyone who wants detailed instructions on how high to turn the grill in order to make toasted cheese will find it useless. It is for people who can be perfectly competent traditional cooks when they wish, but who feel that they may well go berserk if, after a long and tiring day, anyone expects them to spend more than a few minutes of their time and energy cooking.

In the 1950s and 1960s it was the fashion to cook the 'back to nature' and 'old-fashioned' way. Women were encouraged, and were therefore prepared, to bake not only their own bread but their own brioches. They sweated their own vegetables; they marinated for several days; they chopped and peeled and grated by hand; they worried as they weighed extremely complex ingredients on inaccurate and wobbly scales. They infused, dredged, strained, double-boiled and parboiled, clarified and leavened; they cut bloody raw meat into segments; they blanched, basted, chined, piped and stiffened, and they took the beards off mussels. They were quite ready to embark on dishes so ambitious that the culinary procedures involved took up the best part of the day.

Now, in the 1980s, they are all in a state of mutiny. They recognise cookery to be an art, but they find it an art which becomes increasingly personally unfulfilling.

All the people we have spoken to are perfectionists in the sense that they still want the food they serve to be very good – many of them are unliberated enough to admit that they like their food to be praised. But now they seem rather to enjoy praise which they can receive tongue-in-cheek, feeling that they deserve applause not because they have masochistically slogged and slaved, but because they have cleverly cheated.

All the recipes we have included in this book are extremely simple. We have deliberately excluded many dishes, however delicious, which create work, anxiety and mess for the cook. We have also tried to simplify our instructions. There is nothing more dispiriting than staring – before one has even begun cooking – at a recipe which starts in some such way as: '*Effilez en fines lamelles des amandes émondées. Passez la sauce à l'étamine chinoise.*'

Any woman who has spent the day looking after small children, working at a taxing job, doing anything that interests her more than cooking, wants to relax in the evenings. If she entertains she wants to be free to drink and talk to her friends without worrying whether the dinner she is about to produce will be a catastrophe.

Dishes that require her presence in the kitchen – that require her loving surveillance in case they burn, curdle, sink or shrivel, or go wrong in some other unspeakable way, we cannot recommend. Neither do we recommend food whose success is dependent on scrupulous timing. Guests are frequently late, and they often want to drink for an indefinite amount of time as well, before they eat.

Few modern women wish to stay in lonely exile in the kitchen feeling bitter, tense and nerve-wracked as they gaze with exhausted eyes at the lengthy and incomprehensible directions of a recipe which has been written in densely obscure cookery-book jargon, while next door they hear the buzz of talk and laughter.

If friends come into the kitchen and offer their help and company to the cook, they tend to increase her dismay and panic. They get in the way. They don't understand what she expects them to do. They stand with their backs to the cutlery drawer, or lean against the oven. They don't know where the spoons, the sugar, the garlic are. Their embarrassed ineptitude worries her every bit as much as the eventual outcome of her challenging and problematical dish.

Any cook who entertains in the kitchen is beset by similar problems. Many women find it frightening to cook in front of an audience. Should things go amiss, for example – if the butter drops on the floor, they can pick it up and use it, while they are unobserved. Watched by guests, they often throw it away, since they are so intimidated by a fear of their friends' disgust at their slovenly ways.

It is especially important that the cook who plans to do 'public cooking' only ever tries to produce dishes which present no possibility of error. It is harrowing for both the cook and her friends if an intricate sauce boils over; if something burns and makes a revolting smell.

Equally if she is cheating outrageously the cheating should take place before the arrival of her guests, i.e., the cans should be opened and hidden and their contents should be in a baking dish or saucepan, so that they retain prestige and mystery.

Throughout history the drudgery of cooking has been done exclusively by those in subordinate positions. For the most part it has been done by women, whether by the peasant grinding her corn or by the 'Upstairs Downstairs' type cook enslaved by the rigours of formal household etiquette, or by the modern housewife. Although many more men are now cooking, all over the world the situation remains basically the same.

Today, as women take on more and more varying responsibilities, they find the burden of producing meals increasingly irksome. They resent spending hours in the kitchen, because they know that their time can be so much more profitably employed. Labour-saving devices like the Magimix are expensive, but they should never be seen as an extravagance. They are a good investment for anyone who feels her time is precious.

Some of the dishes we suggest are not suitable for serving day after day. A few are expensive, and these are for occasions when you want to produce impressive and delicious food and feel it is worth spending money rather than time.

Some of the recipes that we suggest need only ten minutes' preparation. Some need only two. We have looked for recipes that are unusual and glamorous and taste and look as if they have taken hours.

Some of the things we suggest in the children's section are obviously unsuitable for everyday use. These dishes are meant for parties, for surprises, for moments when a whole lot of children turn up unexpectedly at your house and you can't think what to feed them with.

Vatel, *maître-d'hôtel* of Louis XIV, committed suicide on a Friday because the fish failed to arrive. Much later, Escoffier was asked whether, in that calamitous situation, he too would have taken his life. He shook his head. 'I would have served breasts of chicken and no one would have known the difference.'

- I also have little respect for the over-zealous housewife – the woman who bores you to death with her family affairs, the brilliancy of her children, and her own special methods of cleaning, making pies, darning etc. She is a trial to Society and should neither be encouraged nor welcomed.
  Zara Baar Aronson,
  Twentieth Century Cookery Practice
  (c. 1900)

- On entering the kitchen, invariably say, 'Good morning, Cook'.
  Mrs Beeton's *Everyday Cookery and Housekeeping Book*

First Steps

Il n'y a que le premier pas qui coûte.

Madame du Deffand (1697–1780)

The great morning of the world when first God dawned on Chaos.

Percy Bysshe Shelley (1792–1822)
Adonais

I · Ingredients

● Amongst the articles there should be a store of tea, coffee, Cadbury's cocoa, flour, cornflour, rizine, oatmeal, macaroni, barley, split peas, meat extracts, sauces, essences, vinegars, jams, marmalade, pickles, chutney, mustard, salt, capers, salad oil, baking and egg powders, currants, raisins, candles, beeswax, furniture polish, lamp wicks, emery paper, blacking, night lights, matches and vestas, house-flannel, hearth-stones, and blacklead; also bottles containing the dregs of port wine and sherry, which are most useful in cooking. The bacon should hang on hooks in the ceiling. It is well also to have a pair of scissors hanging on one of the shelves; string, kitchen and lining papers, dessert papers, soufflé cases, cutlet and ham frills should be kept in a drawer.

Mrs de Salis,
The Housewife's Referee (1898)

It is impossible to produce a meal quickly and without anxiety if you run out of salt while you are cooking, or discover at the last moment that there is no oil left for the salad dressing. It is therefore reassuring to have a stock of basic ingredients in your deep freeze, food cupboard and fridge.

Bulk buying can save time, money and effort but needs careful thought. Few families could manage to consume two dozen packets of cornflakes or biscuits before they went soft.

Dried pulses and tinned goods also have a limited shelf life, and many frozen foods begin to deteriorate after between three and six months. Canned, frozen and packed foods give a better result if they are combined with fresh foods. Cream, wine, fresh herbs or grated cheese also improve the taste and add a pure, guileless impression.

- *Varium et mutabile semper.*
  (A fickle thing and changeful is woman always.)

  Virgil (70–19 B.C.)
  Aeneid, iv

Soups

Packeted, dried soups are not recommended. Most canned soups are boring, tasteless or taste unpleasant. Even the most expensive tend to have a curious gluey consistency – owing probably to the presence of corn starch used as a 'filler'. A few, however, are very useful additions to the store cupboard. Various types can be combined (see Quick Bisque, p. 77). Crosse & Blackwell's Vichyssoise and Campbell's consommé are useful bases for other soups, and some brands of oxtail are good provided you add a little tomato purée, a glass of sherry and a squeeze of lemon juice. Home-made cream soups, such as artichoke, celeriac, potato, freeze well.

Meat and Fish

Carving is a time-consuming and tiresome task, and in our view the hot joint is best left for Christmas and purely family occasions. Pork and chicken are the most reliably tender of the quick-cooking meats. Always leave poultry to rest for five to ten minutes in a warm place before carving.

Cold joints are simpler to carve than hot joints and more suitable for a large party than individual steaks and cutlets.

First Steps 17

Very large joints such as hams and turkey can be cooked overnight. Cover the joint closely. Cook in a hot oven for half an hour then leave at lowest setting overnight, say from 10 p.m. to 8 a.m., depending on size. Leave to cool in the pan. Chill before carving. Make absolutely certain that any frozen meat is properly defrosted before beginning to cook.

It is easier to cook a lot of sausages or cutlets in the oven on a rack over a baking tray than to fry or grill them. Fish is also easier to cook in the oven on a well-buttered baking tray, or wrapped loosely, but well sealed, in buttered silver foil. This does away with cooking smells.

A good local delicatessen is a great boon. Most stock a range of cold meats, sausages, pâtés, salads, etc., too wide to go into here in any detail. There are hundreds of varieties of sausage. The small, dried, highly spiced Greek or Spanish sausages make an excellent addition to a cassoulet, or a thick stew of white or red cabbage and lentils. The coarse-cut sausages, such as *saucisson de Toulouse*, are quite different from the usual commercial banger and can be served as a main course with suitably imaginative accompaniments. (Marks and Spencer also sell a good herb-flavoured sausage.) Fresh frankfurters make an almost instant meal steamed and served with potato salad, coleslaw and sweetcorn (or baked beans for children). The coarser Belgian pâtés sold by weight are widely available and suit contemporary taste better than the very smooth *pâtés de foie gras* which usually come in tins, are very expensive and really only suitable for sauces. If you are in any doubt about where to get the best smoked salmon and rollmops look for a kosher shop – try their salt beef too; a delicious change from ordinary cold roast.

Tinned stews, curries, etc., are expensive and on the whole not nice at all, although tinned mince can be used for bolognese sauce. Epicure canned kidneys are useful, and canned ham and tongue are generally good, though expensive.

Tinned luncheon meat is not recommended, although many children are fond of it fried, and regard luncheon meat curry (p. 211) as a treat. But luncheon meat is really only useful on camping holidays miles from civilisation, when normally fastidious people will eat anything: tinned spaghetti, motorway meals – anything.

Although most frozen meat has to be thawed completely before cooking, most fish is best cooked from the frozen state. But frozen fish (or chicken) already battered or breadcrumbed is seldom satisfactory. The coating tends to go soggy.

Canned salmon, tuna, anchovies, sardines, pilchards are well worth keeping in the larder for quick pâtés, salads, fish cakes and kedgerees. Tinned shrimps are tasteless on their own. Mix them with other things. Peeled frozen prawns and shrimps also tend to be tasteless and are best served hot with other ingredients. Frozen crab is rather watery, but can be used in a soup. Canned crab is better – and the addition of a little brandy and cream greatly enhances its flavour.

Rice and Pasta

The easiest way to cook long grain rice is to heat a little oil and fry the rice in it until it is hot, stirring all the time and making sure it doesn't turn brown – about three minutes. Then add $1\frac{1}{2}$ times the quantity of water and some salt, and boil without a cover until almost all the liquid is absorbed. Take off the heat, put a firm lid on it and let it stand for ten minutes. If you like rice fluffier, add twice or even $2\frac{1}{2}$ times the quantity of liquid to rice, so that it can swell more. The amount of liquid and the length of cooking time determine the consistency of rice, while the oil prevents it from sticking together. Cooked rice freezes well. Reheat in a steamer, over boiling water.

Big pans with plenty of boiling water are essential for cooking all pasta. Add a drop or two of oil to prevent boiling over. Pasta cooks no more quickly than new potatoes, but at least it needs no washing or peeling. Cooked pasta does not freeze well except in already made dishes, such as lasagne.

Noodles cook more quickly than other types of pasta and make a good fast accompaniment to veal, pork or chicken with a garlicky butter or cream sauce. They come in a great variety of shapes and with added spinach are a pretty green. Children love vermicelli or alphabet shapes in broth.

There is an English tendency rather to despise macaroni. Nevertheless macaroni cheese (which freezes well) is an extremely comforting and filling dish with a salad or green vegetable. Quick-cooking Quaker macaroni is ready in seven minutes.

Vegetables

Never buy ready washed vegetables unless you are going to use them at once. If you buy potatoes, carrots or other root vegetables in bulk – and if you have a large family and access to country growers this will save you money – make sure they are really dirty, with plenty of earth adhering to them. What you lose in weight is more than compensated for by the way they keep. Store them in a cool dark place and whenever you take any out, look for signs of decay – softness, sprouting or an evil smell – and discard the vegetables responsible. The best time to buy in bulk is late summer and autumn. Stored vegetables start sprouting as spring approaches.

Certain vegetables such as spinach, green beans and peas, freeze very well, while others like sprouts, cauliflower or celery don't. Frozen chips can be bought in bulk. Obviously vegetables which take no trouble to prepare, like courgettes, fennel or broccoli, are better bought fresh than frozen. Dried onions give soups, stews and sauces a good strong flavour, but fresh onions are still best for improving the taste of frozen or canned food. (Fried onions with tomato and peppers – canned peppers are good – make an easy and quick vegetable sauce accompaniment for grilled meat.) Canned flageolet beans and petits pois without artificial colouring are very good, but English canned peas are too green to be wholesome. Frozen mixed vegetables are useful for some stews and curries. Dried mixed vegetables dress up soups such as minestrone. Dried mushrooms are much more flavourful than fresh.

Canned tomatoes are extremely useful for sauces and soups. Celery and artichoke hearts and asparagus do not respond well to canning and are impossible to pass off as fresh except blended in a soup or heated in a made-up dish. Canned mushrooms are good drained well and fried. Canned carrots need dressing up with a glaze of butter, sugar and salt. Canned sweetcorn can be mixed into rice dishes, or soups, and is good with frankfurters. Pickled baby beets and gherkins are a useful standby to brighten up dishes of cold meats and to decorate salads.

After trying out innumerable brands of tinned potatoes we have still not found any that taste remotely like fresh potatoes. It is difficult to think of any purpose to which they could be put. Instant mash has improved over the years. Cadbury's Smash, Wondermash, Sainsbury's or St Michael's instant mash are all good if you cheat a little. Make them creamier by substituting single cream for some of the water. Unlike Cadbury's Smash or Wondermash, the instant mash that comes in the form of powder is inclined to be liquid and limp, so use a little less liquid than indicated on the packet. A few spoonfuls of real left-over potato give instant mash a deceptively genuine taste and texture.

As raw vegetables are very much more nutritious than cooked, and also quicker and easier to prepare, it pays to consider ways of presenting them. Cabbage, sprouts, celeriac, carrots, etc. need to be very thinly sliced or grated. Many children who won't even look at cooked cabbage or spinach will eat coleslaw or shredded spinach salad. Some stores sell prepared raw salads, washed watercress and bean shoots. Nasturtium, sorrel and dandelion leaves make delicious and unusual additions to salads. Wash *very* carefully if there is any chance that they have been sprayed with herbicide or insecticide.

Fresh vegetables can be served as a separate course with melted butter or a hollandaise sauce. Mange-tout peas are familiar to most people, but young broad beans are also delicious cooked in their pods and served with lemon and butter.

First Steps 21

Fruit

Some canned fruits like peaches, or fruit cocktail, are only acceptable to children, but those such as Fortnum and Mason's bottled peaches in brandy are splendid for special occasions and canned, chilled mango, lychees, passion fruit all make a pleasant finish to a meal. Add a liqueur to give the impression that you have taken trouble. Some soft fruits such as raspberries, blackberries, blackcurrants, gooseberries are not spoiled by canning and are useful for quickly prepared fools or trifles, but nearly all soft fruits are better frozen than canned. Strawberries, whether canned or frozen, are soggy and unappetising.

Dried apricots soaked overnight and then cooked slowly in the oven are delicious, and prunes similarly treated, stoned, puréed and chilled are unrecognisable served with a dash of slivovic and whipped cream.

Fresh fruit in season – peaches, apricots, plums – make a beautiful centre piece and a lovely dessert, especially if you decorate them with leaves – geranium, vine or ivy.

Pastry, Bread and Cake

Buy frozen vol-au-vent and flan cases (we include a recipe for quick puff pastry on p. 60; but it still has to be rolled out once). Jus-Rol pastry is good – it too has to be rolled out, but is virtually foolproof. The various packeted dry mixes for pastry and dumplings are rather pointless if you have an electric mixer. What you want to avoid is the messy and time-consuming task of rubbing fat into flour with the icy tips of the fingers.

Bread mixes or prepared dough are only useful if you intend serving hot rolls with soup or pâté. If you are lucky enough to have a local baker, you needn't bother with all this. You can warm up 'French' bread (in this country it is not very like the bread eaten in France but is still edible). The easiest way to prepare garlic bread is to slice the loaf lengthways, rather than in vertical chunks, and then spread both cut sides with your garlic butter, wrap in foil, heat in the oven and cut at the table. If you are serving a few people you can toast garlic-buttered slices of bread under the grill.

Rolls and buns can be moistened with a little milk and water and warmed in the oven. French bread can be improved by brushing with a beaten egg, sprinkling with sesame or poppy seeds and heating through in the oven.

Pitta bread – the unleavened 'pocketed' bread of Greece and the Middle East – can be heated to dip into purées such as hummus, or taramasalata (pp. 168, 61). Or you can fill it with hamburger and salad for children, or make an instant pizza (p. 209). All these breads freeze well.

Sliced bread is a useful invention, so it is a pity it is so horrible in most cases. Look for a baker who slices his own bread.

Making breadcrumbs is easy with a food processor. Most brands on the market coat everything in an orange mess that looks chemical and doesn't taste of bread. Krucks Natural Bread Crumbs are an exception and are sold in sensibly large cartons. Breadcrumbs can be kept in plastic bags in the freezer, or in a screw-topped jar if previously baked.

Instant cake mixes can be useful both for producing cakes quickly and for helping to keep children quiet on wet afternoons. Most can be prepared in a mixer since few ingredients, usually only an egg, have to be added.

Sainsbury's, Marks and Spencer's and other large firms sell 'boudoir' biscuits, sponge and madeira cake which are ideal for many puddings. Many bakers sell 'blind' flan cases.

Milk, Cream, Yoghourt

Always keep dried, and tinned evaporated milk. They are horrid in coffee or tea but invaluable for sauces and puddings. Evaporated milk is perfectly good in quiches, etc.

Heavy double and clotted cream freeze well. Tinned cream is useful for cooking.

Yoghourt is a good and slimming substitute for cream in many recipes, and does freeze.

Butter, Margarine

Butter can be frozen. Keep both salted and unsalted, the latter for butter creams and hard sauces. Soft margarine is invaluable if for some reason you have to make a lot of sandwiches. Spread thinly. It helps to keep the bread moist, and while you don't get the pleasure of butter you are spared the nastiness of hard margarine. If you must use butter, cream it first.

No one with any sense has bothered for years now with the wooden bats that make butter into little fluted curls, but those rectangular slabs are a bit boring, and many shops sell half-pound round pats decorated with cows, or whatever, in low relief.

Cheese

Gratin dishes are more interesting with cheese on top, and pasta can be served with almost anything – from bolognese sauce to butter alone – as long as you have plenty of freshly grated cheese to sprinkle over it. While Parmesan is, of course, the best cheese for pasta, Gruyère melts better into a golden crust on open casseroles because of its fat content. If either of these cheeses is unavailable or too expensive, Cheddar will do instead, and a combination of Cheddar and Parmesan is the best of all. Cottage cheese is a slimming (and cheap) substitute for cream cheese.

Cream cheese freezes well, but must be used within eight hours of thawing or it becomes crumbly. Most good delicatessens sell Stilton in jars – actually more economical than the large cheeses as there is very little waste and no controversy over the relative merits of spooning and slicing (if you *have* a large Stilton, slice it, keeping the surface as level as possible).

Freshly grated cheese is best, but you can buy ready-grated Parmesan, and grated Cheddar in plastic bags can be kept in the freezer. Always wrap cheese in clinging plastic if you keep it in the fridge. Never buy more than you need of Brie, Camembert, etc. They have no left-over value at all once they have dried out.

In the summer add fresh chopped herbs or garlic to cream or cottage cheese – much cheaper than the bought 'herb' cheeses. The Greek fetta, pounded with oil and garlic, is delicious with hot pitta bread.

Oils

The flavour of other oils cannot compare with that of olive oil for making salad dressings or for tossing spaghetti. It is thicker and more substantial too, so you use less. It may be blended with a bland oil to make it go further.

Corn oil is the most widely used for frying and other

methods of cooking. Do not use 'vegetable' oil – it generally tastes horrible. Walnut, sunflower, safflower, sesame oils, are all unrefined (cold-pressed are best), have distinctive flavours and may be used for special dishes.

Oil and vinegar can be flavoured with garlic, tarragon or other herbs. Put your garlic or herbs in a bottle with the oil or vinegar, stopper closely and keep for a few weeks before using.

Herbs and Spices

Dried herbs that have accumulated in the kitchen over the years, gone grey with age and taste like sawdust should be thrown out. Dried bay leaves, thyme and marjoram keep relatively better than others; but many frozen herbs are as good as fresh herbs and can be kept for a few months as they take up no space in a freezer or in the freezing compartment of the fridge – be careful to seal them properly. Fresh parsley and mint keep well in a screw-topped jar in the fridge with their stalks in a little water.

Avoid garlic substitutes, as they don't taste like garlic. It isn't necessary to peel a clove of garlic before you crush it in the garlic press; just cut off both ends.

A tiny pinch of monosodium glutamate enhances flavour astonishingly but has been known to have side effects – giddiness, numbness – so use sparingly.

Nutmeg, ginger, cinnamon sticks, cloves are all easily stored and are better kept in their original form – dried, rather than powdered. Keep a vanilla pod and dried orange peel in screw-topped jars of caster sugar to flavour puddings, cream, ices, etc.*

Black and white peppercorns, juniper berries, dried chillies

---

* If you find you have no caster sugar, put ordinary granulated into the food processor and blend until it is as fine as you wish – about half a minute should do for a small quantity. (This is a good idea anyway as caster costs considerably more than granulated sugar.)

all keep well in closely stoppered jars.

Keep paprika and cayenne pepper. Curry powder should be mixed to a paste with water before adding to the other ingredients. A pinch of saffron can do wonders for a dullish risotto or fish soup. Cumin, coriander, cardamom, fenugreek, fennel seeds, star anise are all worth keeping.

Sauces and Relishes

Keep white and red wine and cider vinegar, and a stock of tabasco, soy sauce and tomato purée. Whisky (malt) is a good substitute for brandy in many savoury sauces, and gin (because of the juniper flavour) is good with some pork dishes. Cider is good with fish in place of white wine.

Bottled mint sauce is perfectly acceptable – add white wine vinegar and sugar. Dried mint is no good. Worcestershire sauce is a great help in dressing up such items as tinned mince, and mushroom ketchup is an excellent flavouring – especially with forced mushrooms, which can taste slightly insipid. Tomato ketchup is useful if you wish your children to eat regularly. Heinz's contains no colouring or additives and helps down many a chop or fish finger.

Buy chutney and pickles from Oriental shops – there are many delicious varieties. Avoid most English brands except Sharwood's. Gentleman's Relish and Marmite are good on toast under scrambled egg, grilled tomatoes or mushrooms.

There are many good types of French ready-made mustard, such as Dijon, with a variety of herbs and flavourings added. English ready-made mustard is generally too salty. (If you wish to keep English mustard you have made yourself, add a *little* salt, cover and keep in the fridge.)

Use Koch Brand or Kühne grated horseradish. It tastes absolutely fresh and keeps for a long time in the fridge or freezer. Mix it with cream and serve it with hot or cold beef or smoked mackerel, or trout. (Make it milder for fish.)

Home-made mayonnaise is always best, and easy to make

in a blender. (Put a scant teaspoon of dry mustard in with the egg yolks to help the coalescing.) But Hellman's is a good substitute. It can be improved by blending or stirring in an egg yolk and more oil. This makes it richer and yellower and is still easier than starting from scratch. Salad without mayonnaise is better than salad with certain so-called 'mayonnaises'. Most bottled 'dressings' are not nice either.

Firms such as Colman's make a variety of packeted, dried sauces – white, cheese, bread, parsley, etc. These are a useful short cut, but it is a good idea to add more butter, a little nutmeg, or grated onion to emphasise the flavour. The widely advertised tinned sauces which are intended to metamorphosise any stew into *boeuf bourguignon*, goulash, etc., are on the whole an expensive waste of time if you have at hand a selection of spices, herbs, some left-over wine, and cream.

One good idea of the *nouvelle cuisine* is something the English thought of during the war and then forgot as cream and white flour became available again. Purées of vegetables make excellent non-fattening sauces. Grated carrot with a little chopped onion and perhaps a dash of Marmite, simmered until tender in as little water as possible and then blended, makes a good accompaniment to grilled sausages or steak. Steamed fennel, or celery and lettuce hearts, steamed, seasoned and blended, are good with white fish instead of the usual buttery sauces.

Canned tomatoes should always be simmered until well reduced before they are added to flans or to casseroles, unless they are the only liquid ingredient you are using.

Stock Cubes

Instant stock should only be made with carefully selected stock cubes – some brands smother the natural flavour of the dish. Knorr is good, and the kosher and vegetable varieties that are now available. A stew or casserole can be improved by simply adding a good stock cube rather than by throwing in dried and indistinguishable herbs. Shun all 'gravy' powders

and mixes, except for those composed only of salt and caramel.

Stuffings

Instant stuffings – sage and onion and parsley and thyme – are good. Mix both with a diluted stock cube, or home-made gravy, rather than plain water. Add a little sherry and some lemon zest to the parsley and thyme.

Jellies and Jams

The best jams – apart from the very expensive English brands – are those that come from Poland and Hungary and are made purely from fruit and sugar. Plum jam is good with pork. Redcurrant jelly for lamb can be improved by a little port or madeira. Tinned apple sauce (the sort they make for babies will do) is better for the addition of a little lemon juice and zest.

Left-overs

If you have good food you have good left-overs. The remains of a joint are almost always best served cold (there is something not at all glamorous about rissoles and hash réchauffé).

Slice the meat very thinly and arrange it on a plate with olives, onion rings, sliced peppers or whatever you have. If your left-over potatoes have been buttered, sauté them. If not, serve cold with mayonnaise. Add a green or tomato salad, or green bean salad (p. 171). Make sure the table looks pretty and no one will suspect this meal of being yesterday's dinner. Or make a salmagundy – a salad of sliced cold meat arranged in layers in a bowl with potatoes, hard-boiled eggs, beetroot, anchovies – anything. Pour over a vinaigrette and sprinkle with parsley.

Left-over roast beef can be cleverly disguised in lasagne. Mince the meat, fry one or two chopped onions and a few cloves of garlic. Mix them all together with a good squeeze of tomato purée and a pinch of basil. Cook the sheets of pasta carefully and layer them alternately with the meat mixture. Pour over a well flavoured cheese sauce. Sprinkle with grated cheese and cook in a moderate oven until warmed through. Do not overheat as this will toughen the meat. Bubble the top under the grill. Roast lamb can be similarly treated – substitute fried or steamed slices of aubergine for the pasta, and you have moussaka.

With the aid of a blender the most unexpected ingredients can be converted into soup – left-over cauliflower or macaroni cheese, for example, blended with a stock cube and milk and water and served very hot. Have regard to the colour of left-over vegetables; most mix as a soup quite contentedly but it would be a pity to put tomatoes or carrots with a green vegetable. Sprouts, spinach, beans, cabbage all make delicious soup with gravy or stock or cream added. Add a teaspoonful of curry powder to carrot soup.

If people ask what kind of soup they are eating, say it's an old family recipe.

Final Tip

Never go shopping when you are hungry: you will buy far more than you need.

> Common Sense is the most widely shared commodity in the world, for every man is convinced that he is well supplied with it.
>
> René Descartes (1596–1650)
> *Le Discours de la Méthode*

II · Gadgets

People who value their time and have realised that work in the kitchen should be rationalised in the same way as work in an office or a factory won't need any tips on gadgets. They will have found out long ago which suit them best.

Those who find kitchen gadgets 'gimmicky' and take pride in doing everything in the old-fashioned, 'proper' way probably don't have to cook regular meals for large families. Others may have got so bored with the endless kitchen routine that they can no longer be bothered to keep up with modern gadgets. One woman felt so guilty about the waste of electricity when she looked into her empty fridge that she unplugged it in a final gesture of 'cook's despair'.

Many kitchen gadgets can be bought at the David Mellor Shop, 4 Sloane Square, London S.W.1. Goods at Habitat – now in operation from twenty-seven stores in Britain – range from peppermills to sofas and include electrical appliances. Both shops have mail-order services, and their illustrated catalogues can be ordered by post.

It is a good idea to keep a set of *measuring spoons* in the kitchen (although as an experienced cook you will probably use one only, when you make dishes that require very precise amounts of an ingredient, such as gelatine). They are made of coloured plastic and cost next to nothing.

First Steps 31

There is no need for expensive scales. A *cook's measure*, made of clear plastic, will measure solids and liquids and can be washed like an ordinary jug.

A *wall can opener* is much handier than the ordinary tin opener. The Prestige model comes in two parts. You can slide the opener off the bracket on the wall and wash it regularly – this is important as residual traces of food can decay and cause food poisoning.

The most neglected, and yet the most necessary, kitchen tool is a *sharp knife*. Ideally, razor-sharp knives should hang on a magnetic band on the wall. Stainless steel is easier to maintain than carbon steel, which discolours quickly. On the other hand, it is easier to keep the softer carbon steel sharp. Weighing up one against the other, stainless steel is probably the more useful, provided you buy the very best quality. *Deep freeze knives* can be bought at most good stores. An *electric carving knife* is useful for very large joints.

The *Mouli-parsmint* is useful for chopping herbs. The *Mouli-grater* grates cheese, carrots and chocolate. French cooks have always used the *mandoline*. The best is the Waefa Universal Slicer from Switzerland, which consists of a wooden frame and two adjustable steel blades, one smooth and one corrugated. It is not only much faster than cutting by hand, but you can cut vegetables such as cucumbers more thinly.

The Westmark Biopress *garlic press*, in die-cast aluminium, is probably the best. Its shallowness and simple rectangular design facilitate easy cleaning.

A *salad spinner* is cheap and very useful. Swinging lettuce leaves in wire baskets or drying them in glass-cloths, from which they will emerge limp and tired, is no longer necessary. The lettuce is simply spun in a plastic bowl, which fits into another bowl. If you are very careful you can put your salad in the spin dryer. Place it in a clean pillow case and give it one very brief whirl.

The *terracotta potato baker*, the *chicken brick*, and the *fish brick* are the only traditional pots we have singled out as particularly useful from a variety of pots and pans too vast to describe here. These unglazed pots bake food in its own juices, which preserves the aroma. While they don't speed up the actual cooking process, they save a lot of trouble. The food does not dry out and you need add no liquid or fat, only seasoning and herbs or vegetables. They should not be washed with detergent: just rinse well in hot water.

The *wok*, or Chinese frying pan, is coming into use more and more in Europe as people have begun to appreciate the subtlety of quick stir-frying, which brings out the flavour of the food while retaining the texture, and is the quickest and easiest way of cooking. David Mellor sells a well finished *wok*, which is made in England. It comes in two sizes with a matching *wok-tan*, or Chinese stirring spoon.

A *pressure cooker* cooks food in a fraction of the time it would take in an ordinary pan. There is no reason to be afraid of this gadget any longer, and no need to rush across the kitchen to hold it under the cold tap at the end of cooking. The Tefal pressure cooker can be opened while still under pressure without running cold water on it. It comes in three sizes (eight pint, ten pint and fourteen pint) and has a three-way food divider and wire basket, so that you can cook meat, potatoes and vegetables all at the same time.

The *slow cooker* is invaluable for people who are out all day. You can put a meal in it in the morning and forget about it until you return in the evening. Most slow cookers have a removable glazed stoneware bowl in which you can serve the food and then wash it like other dishes. The bowl sits in an outer casing which contains the element. The food cooks gently for hours at a very low and even temperature. There is hardly any evaporation or loss of juices, and the food will never burn.

An oven with an *automatic timing device* for starting and stopping cooking is also useful for full-time workers. The food is prepared in the usual way and left to cook in the oven for the desired time during the day.

People who have an *Aga* would never cook by any other method. Agas run on gas or solid fuel are expensive to buy but economical once installed. Food can be roasted, grilled or fried in the hot oven without releasing any cooking smells or fumes and the slow oven cooks stews, casseroles, etc. to perfection with no risk of failure. It is extraordinary how much time is saved by having an oven in constant readiness and always at the correct temperature for anything from minute steak to meringues.

The *microwave oven* is a luxury. It is not meant to replace conventional ovens but to complement them. It saves fuel, food and time, reheating food in seconds and cooking it in about one-fifth of the time taken by traditional cooking. Defrosting food in a microwave oven only takes minutes. Food can be cooked in the dishes in which it is to be served, provided they are not made of metal, as they remain cool throughout the cooking process. Nobody would be lost without one, but a microwave oven is a useful short cut. The Toshiba is the most reliable and widely sold brand in Britain.

An *infra-red grill* cooks food between two ribbed hotplates. This is ideal for steaks, chops and cutlets, as their juices are sealed in in a fraction of the time it would take under an ordinary grill or in a frying pan. Fat need not be added and shrinking of meat is reduced to a minimum. The Sona grill has a particularly neat design. Its self-levelling hinges adjust to accommodate food to almost two inches deep, including cakes, biscuits and pies. It will cook steak straight from the freezer and leave it brown and crisp.

Mixers, blenders and food processors save an enormous amount of time. Of all the products on the market we have found the Magimix, the Moulinex Maxima and the Kenwood Chef to be the most useful and versatile.

On the whole the Kenwood Chef is most suitable for larger families, for people who do a lot of baking. It has a capacious mixing bowl, three beaters – for dough, other mixtures, and egg whites and cream – and a number of useful attachments, including an efficient potato peeler, a mincer, slicer, and grater, coffee and grain mills, a liquidiser and a surprising attachment that turns butter back into cream against all the dictates of the second law of thermodynamics.

Food processors such as the Magimix and the Moulinex Maxima are designed on different principles from mixers. They have two blades, slicing and grating attachments and a juicer, are very fast, relatively quiet and offer by far the best method of making meat and fish pâtés, vegetable purées, etc. Their sharp blade chops food and gives a better result than a mincer. With the plastic blade they make superb mayonnaises, sauces and dressings in no time at all. The Moulinex Maxima now also has a whisking attachment which will whip cream and egg whites, and mash potatoes.

Automatic toasters are useful. The Morphy Richards 4409 (U.K.) and the Sunbeam TO41 (West Germany) are to be recommended. The latter takes four slices of bread and costs only a few pounds more than the two-slice toasters.

The electric Melitta Automat 131 is an untroublesome and economical *coffee-making machine.* It keeps the coffee hot without boiling it and doesn't make it bitter. You can make the coffee in advance and it is ready to serve whenever you need it.

The greatest cause for anxiety before a meal is keeping the food hot. The best way out of this dilemma, if you can afford it and if you don't own an Aga, is to buy a *hot tray*. Salton's hot trays come in a variety of sizes, are well made, though not exactly beautiful, and last many years. They incorporate little hot circles, or H spots, to stand coffee pots on. Salton's have recently built these heated trays into trolleys, as well as coffee tables. A more expensive alternative for frequent and big dinner parties is a Kay-met hot cabinet. This is a complete cupboard with a heating oven and keep-warm compartment for vegetables.

III · Measurements

It will be evident in many of the following recipes that the people who contributed them are so practised in their preparation that they know by instinct and at a glance how much of each ingredient they will need. It is seldom allowed by the authors of cookery books that much leeway is possible, but most harassed, experienced cooks work perfectly well on educated guesswork. However, for the timorous we append the following list.

Liquids
1 fluid oz = 2 tablespoons
10 fluid oz = ½ pint = ¼ litre

1 mug or breakfast cup = ½ pint = ¼ litre
1 teacup = ¼ pint = ⅛ litre

Jam
1 tablespoon = 2 oz

Flour, Sugar
1 rounded dessertspoon = ½ oz = 14 gm
1 rounded tablespoon = 1 oz = 28 gm
1 level teacup = 4 oz = 112 gm

Breadcrumbs
1 heaped tablespoon = ½ oz

Rice
1 heaped tablespoon = 1 oz
1 level teacup = 4 oz

Lump sugar
6 lumps = 1 oz

American measures
8 fluid oz = 1 American cup
1 oz butter = 2 American tablespoons
1 oz flour = 2 rounded American tablespoons

IV · Presentation and panache

Angst and panic are the cook's worst enemies. It is possible to exaggerate the expectations of one's guests to a point where caviar and lobster thermidor washed down by vintage champagne no longer seem good enough. *Larousse gastronomique*, *haute cuisine* cookery writers, the intimidating and time-consuming *cuisine minceur*, can paralyse the cook as they take over the role of a ferociously unappeasable culinary super ego.

Presentation is important

If the cook believes her food is good, her belief, like faith, can move mountains and her confidence will percolate through to her guests and reassure them. This is particularly true if on arrival they have been given strong exotic cocktails (see pp. 39–54). Cocktails can create an illusion that trouble has been taken. There is something gay and pleasant in being greeted by a relaxed hostess with a cocktail shaker in her hand. If you have arms there is no reason to use the new American cocktail shaker which operates on a battery. The avoidance of trouble can sometimes be carried to excess.

Whatever you decide to serve, never say that it would have been better if you had been able to get hold of some fresh angelica. Never on any account say that your dish seemed to taste much more delicious when you cooked it last week. Modesty is unbecoming in a cook and only stimulates the critical faculties of guests, the very faculties which should ideally be deadened by the plying of cocktails and good wine.*

- Dinner began with tea and bean flourcakes, passed on to fish served on little mats of grass, went on to soup served in lacquered bowls, proceeded to prawns, halted, hesitated, and went back to soup, scratched its head, so to speak, and then, as if with an after-thought, served up a quail, apologized for the substantiality of the quail by presenting a salted plum on a little plate, and then harked shamelessly back to soup, ending deliriously with a shower of little dishes containing everything conceivable, and a big bowl of rice.

This is an impressionist picture of a Japanese dinner.
The Crimson Azaleas
H. De Vere Stacpoole, (1908)

---

* We have served inferior wine in lordly bottles and got away with it. This is to do with expectation and effect. For instance, if you blindfold someone, tell him he is drinking coffee and give him tea he will find it difficult to tell the difference, and if you gave a person pink-coloured spinach, even if the taste were unimpaired, he wouldn't know what he was eating. Still it is a dirty trick, and only for the quite unscrupulous.

Cocktails

> The difficulty lies not in the use of a bad thing but in the abuse of a very good thing.
>
> Abraham Lincoln (1809–65)

Measurements and Accessories

A gill is a quarter of a pint and the tops of most cocktail shakers hold ¼ gill.

For skilful cocktail making you will need: A cocktail shaker, a mixing glass, a long-handled silver spoon for stirring, a strainer, lemon and orange squeezer, lime squeezer, ice bag and mallet for breaking ice, a wooden pestle and a bitters dasher (or dasher top for bitters bottle).

The syrup required in some recipes is a simple syrup made by boiling 1 lb sugar in 1 pint water.

Shaking should be brisk and the shaker held with both hands until the ingredients are thoroughly mixed and cooled; do not shake for so long that the ice melts and makes the drink watery.

Unless a recipe calls for 'gentle' stirring, this should also be done quite briskly by whirling the mixing spoon round.

As in all recipes, the proportions for mixing cocktails will vary according to taste and experiment.

Cool, Fruity Summer Drinks

Tequila Sunrise

⅓ gill Tequila
⅔ gill orange juice

1 dash of grenadine

Half fill a cocktail shaker with broken ice, add Tequila and orange juice, shake well and strain into a glass. Add a dash of grenadine and serve with straws.

Luigi

A few drops of Cointreau
¼ gill French vermouth
¼ gill gin

2 or 3 dashes of grenadine
The juice of half an orange
1 dash of orange zest

Half fill the shaker with broken ice and add the French vermouth, followed by the Cointreau, the gin, the orange juice and the grenadine. Shake well and strain into a glass. Serve with a dash of orange zest on top. (Most good hardware stores now stock a little gadget like a claw with a handle, for scraping orange or lemon zest.)

Mardi Gras

¼ gill whisky
1 dash Pernod
2 dashes of Peychaud Bitters

2 dashes of Angostura Bitters
1 lump of sugar
1 twist of lemon

Into a heavy mixing glass put the sugar, Peychaud Bitters and Angostura Bitters. Add the whisky and half fill with broken ice. Now put into a chilled cocktail glass the dash of Pernod, roll round glass and throw away. Into this glass strain mixture from mixing glass, squeeze a twist of lemon on top and serve.

Ward 9

1 teaspoon grenadine
¼ gill orange juice

¼ gill lemon juice
½ gill whisky

Half fill shaker with broken ice, add ingredients, shake well and strain into a cocktail glass.

Daiquiri

$\frac{1}{3}$ gill lime juice $\qquad$ $\frac{1}{6}$ gill rum
1 or 2 dashes of grenadine

Half fill the shaker with broken ice and add the lime juice. Then add the rum and grenadine. Shake well and strain into a cocktail glass.

Fizzes

Except for Buck's Fizz, these are all prepared in the shaker, half filled with broken ice. Having strained the ingredients from the shaker into a tall glass, fill up with soda water and serve. Here are just a few:

Gin Fizz

1 teaspoon sugar syrup $\qquad$ $\frac{3}{4}$ gill dry gin
Juice of 1 lemon, or juice of
  $\frac{1}{2}$ a lemon and $\frac{1}{2}$ a lime

Rum Fizz

As Gin Fizz but using rum

Brandy Fizz

$\frac{3}{4}$ gill lemon juice $\qquad$ 1 egg white
5 or 6 dashes of grenadine $\qquad$ $\frac{1}{2}$ gill brandy
1 teaspoon brown curaçao

Buck's Fizz

Equal quantities of champagne and fresh orange juice

Coolers

These are prepared in a tall glass with one lump of ice and stirred well.

Bulldog Cooler

1 or 2 dashes of sugar syrup
Juice of $\frac{1}{2}$ an orange
$\frac{1}{2}$ gill dry gin
$\frac{1}{3}$ pint ginger ale
Orange zest

Stir well, squeeze a little orange zest on top and serve.

Whisky Cooler

2 dashes of orange bitters
$\frac{1}{2}$ gill Scotch whisky
$\frac{1}{2}$ pint soda water
1 slice of orange
1 or 2 dashes of sugar syrup (optional)

Stir well, and serve with a slice of orange. To make a sweeter cocktail one or two dashes of sugar syrup can be added.

Club Cooler

1 dash of lemon juice
$\frac{1}{6}$ gill grenadine
$\frac{1}{3}$ gill Italian vermouth
$\frac{1}{2}$ pint soda water

More Exotic Summer Drinks

- The world is full of care, much like unto a bubble; Women and care, and care and women, and women and care and trouble.

    Rev. Nathaniel Ward (1578–1652)

Mint Juleps

Prepare with brandy, gin, rum or whisky in the following way:

To prepare the julep glass itself, fill it with finely shaved ice and add two or three sprigs of fresh young mint, first dipped in powdered sugar. Decorate with pieces of fruit.

To prepare the julep, dip four sprigs of mint in powdered sugar and add sufficient water to dissolve the sugar (as little as possible). Crush the mint *very gently* to extract flavour. Strain this liquid into a tumbler to which is added broken ice and $\frac{3}{4}$ gill of the chosen spirit. Stir well and strain into the mint julep glass. This cocktail should be served with straws.

More exotic still is *Champagne Julep*. This is made by adding two sprigs of young mint to a tumbler containing one lump of sugar, crushing the mint very gently as before and adding two lumps of ice. Now fill the tumbler with champagne, stir gently and decorate with fruit.

French '76

$\frac{1}{6}$ *gill dry gin*	1 *teaspoon powdered sugar*
1 *dash of lemon juice*	*Champagne*

Pour first three ingredients, mixed, into a champagne glass containing cracked ice and fill with champagne.

Champagne Cocktail

1 gill champagne *A few drops of old brandy*
A few drops of brown curaçao *A few drops of plain syrup*

Have the champagne ready on ice and keep it well corked. Half fill a tumbler with broken ice. Add the curaçao, old brandy, plain syrup and champagne, in that order. Stir well and serve in a large wine glass. One bottle of champagne makes between 6 and 8 cocktails.

Champagne Framboise

1 bottle of champagne *Raspberries*
6 tablespoons of caster sugar *Cracked ice*

Sieve the raspberries and add to the champagne in a glass jug. Stir in the sugar (adding a little more if the raspberries are rather sour). Ice and serve.

Black Velvet

Equal quantities of champagne and Guinness

Colin's Killer

1 bottle of brandy to 6 bottles of sparkling white wine

Serve chilled.

If you use still white wine and add a pound jar of clear honey and stir well, you have something similar to *mulsum*, which the ancient Romans enjoyed.

Cocktails 47

Aperitifs

Listed here are those drinks which, while still extremely pleasant, set a slightly quieter tone.

Dubonnet

$\frac{1}{3}$ gill Dubonnet
$\frac{1}{6}$ gill dry gin
$\frac{1}{2}$ teaspoon orange bitters

Half fill the shaker with broken ice and add the dry gin, then the Dubonnet and the orange bitters. Shake and strain into a cocktail glass.

Martini (Dry)

$\frac{1}{4}$ gill dry gin
$\frac{1}{4}$ gill French vermouth
1 dash of lemon zest

Half fill a tumbler with broken ice and add the dry gin, followed by the French vermouth. Stir well and pass through a strainer into a cocktail glass. Squeeze lemon zest on top.

Martini (Sweet)

$\frac{1}{3}$ gill dry gin
$\frac{1}{6}$ gill Italian vermouth (Martini's)
$\frac{1}{2}$ teaspoon orange bitters
1 or 2 dashes of lemon zest

Half fill a tumbler with broken ice and add the dry gin, followed by the Italian vermouth and the orange bitters. Stir well and strain into a cocktail glass. Squeeze the lemon zest on top.

Highballs

The various bases for Highballs include brandy, gin, rum, whisky, sherry and vermouth, but wines such as claret and aperitif wines may also be used. Here is a recipe for Applejack Highball; the others are all made in the same way.

Add ¾ gill of Applejack Brandy to a tumbler containing one or two lumps of ice. Fill up with soda water or ginger ale and serve with either a slice of lemon or a piece of lemon peel.

Bull Shot

Chilled consommé *Vodka*
Lemon juice *Pepper*

Mix to taste in a tumbler and stir well. This is a good pick-me-up and hangover cure; less cloying than the better known Bloody Mary.

Vermouth Aperitif

⅙ gill brown curaçao *⅓ gill soda water*
⅓ gill French vermouth

Put the brown curaçao in a wine glass and add the French vermouth and soda water. Serve with a small lump of ice.

Creamy Cocktails

Flips

These are classically made with the yolk of an egg, but they are even more delicious made with a whole egg and mixed in an electric blender.

Sherry Flip

Put ½ gill of sweet sherry, an egg and a lump of ice in the blender and blend well. Pour into a wine glass and sprinkle with grated nutmeg.

Flips can also be made with brandy, port, rum and whisky, adding a little sugar where necessary.

Coffee

½ teaspoon sugar
¼ gill port
⅛ gill brandy
1 egg yolk

Half fill a shaker with ice chips and add the egg yolk. Then add sugar, port and brandy and shake until cold. Strain into a wine glass.

Egg Sour

1 egg
¼ gill Cointreau
¼ gill brandy
3 dashes of lemon juice
Sugar or sugar syrup to taste

Shake the ingredients well in a shaker half filled with broken ice and strain into a wine glass. This is an excellent cocktail for those who like creamy concoctions only if they are not too sweet.

Alexander

⅙ gill dry gin
⅙ gill Crème de Cacao
⅙ gill sweet cream

Half fill a shaker with broken ice, add ingredients, shake well and strain into a cocktail glass.

Liz Knights
Banana Daiquiri

This should really be made with banana liqueur, but I have made it very successfully with banana milk shake syrup. Served with straws in a cocktail glass, it looks very exotic.

$\frac{1}{4}$ gill white rum
1 teaspoon banana syrup
　or banana liqueur
3 tablespoons cream

Put the ingredients in the blender with two lumps of ice and blend until frothy.

Miscellaneous Drinks

These are very useful for parties as they can be mixed in large quantities beforehand (but not too long beforehand!).

● The sooner every party breaks up the better.
　　　　　　　　　　　Jane Austen (1775–1817)
　　　　　　　　　　　　　　　Emma

Champagne Cup

1 bottle champagne
$\frac{1}{2}$ gill brandy
$\frac{1}{3}$ gill yellow chartreuse
　or brown curaçao
$\frac{1}{4}$ gill maraschino
$\frac{1}{4}$ gill plain syrup
1 bottle soda water
Slices of orange, lemon,
　cucumber, fresh mint
Pieces of fresh fruit
　(optional)

In a large bowl place a large lump of ice and add the champagne, followed by the brandy, the yellow chartreuse, the maraschino, plain syrup and soda water. Stir well and strain into large tumblers decorated with slices of orange, lemon, cucumber and fresh mint. On top of that can be placed pieces of fresh fruit.

Claret Cup

1 quart claret
$\frac{1}{4}$ gill lemon juice
$\frac{1}{2}$ gill brandy
$\frac{1}{3}$ gill brown curaçao
$\frac{1}{4}$ gill maraschino
$\frac{1}{4}$ gill plain syrup
1 bottle soda water

Make in exactly the same way as Champagne Cup but adding the lemon juice.

Sauternes Cup

1 bottle Sauternes
$\frac{1}{2}$ gill lemon juice
$\frac{1}{8}$ gill grenadine
$\frac{1}{2}$ gill maraschino
$\frac{1}{3}$ gill yellow chartreuse
   (optional)
$\frac{1}{4}$ gill Benedictine
$\frac{1}{2}$ gill brandy
$\frac{1}{4}$ gill brown curaçao
1 pint soda water
Slices of lemon, cucumber,
   fresh fruit

In a large bowl, place a large lump of ice and add the Sauternes. Then the lemon juice, grenadine, brown curaçao, maraschino, yellow chartreuse, Benedictine, brandy and soda water. Stir and strain. Serve decorated with slices of lemon, cucumber and fresh fruit.

Sangria

1 bottle red wine
1 bottle lemonade or $\frac{1}{2}$ bottle lemonade
   and $\frac{1}{2}$ bottle soda water
3 small oranges
1 lemon
Sugar to taste

Quarter the oranges and lemon and place in a large jug. Add about three tablespoons of sugar and gently crush the fruit to extract flavour. Half fill jug with cracked ice and add wine and lemonade. Stir well and serve.

Kir Genia

Mix, to taste, Ribena and red wine.

These last two are good for teenage parties and less intoxicating than the usual cider. It is also a good idea on these occasions to offer a non-alcoholic fruit cup. To a bottle of apple juice and a large carton of grapefruit or orange juice add one bottle of lemonade. Chill well and float sliced fruit on top.

Hot Drinks

These are excellent served on cold nights, either before or after a meal.

Oxford Punch

3 parts rum
2 parts brandy
1 part lemon squash

6 parts boiling water
Sugar to taste

The ingredients should be mixed together well in a punch bowl and served in punch glasses or cups.

Hot Buttered Rum

2 tablespoons rum *2 teaspoons butter*
2 teaspoons sugar *½ teaspoon mixed spices*

Put all the ingredients in a tumbler and fill with boiling water. Stir well.

Rum Toddy

1 teaspoon sugar *Grated nutmeg or*
3 dashes of lime juice *powdered cinnamon*
¾ gill rum

Dissolve the sugar and hot water and add the lime juice and rum. Fill up with boiling water and serve topped with grated nutmeg or powdered cinnamon.

Whisky Toddy

1 teaspoon sugar *Slice of lemon*
¾ gill whisky

Dissolve the sugar in hot water and add the whisky. Fill up with boiling water and serve topped with a slice of lemon.

First Courses

> There are two classes of hors-d'oeuvre, plain and dressed. The most popular and highly esteemed hors d'oeuvre are oysters when in season, which is for eight months (all the months in which there is an 'r'); they are known as the 'king of hors-d'oeuvre'. Next in popularity to the oyster comes caviar.
>
> *The New Century Cookery Book* (1904)

Oysters

Oysters are wildly expensive and a nuisance to open. Try tinned, smoked oysters – chilled on hot toast, or with thin brown bread and butter and slices of lemon. Or stir them into a bowl of mixed yoghourt and whipped cream lightly flavoured with horseradish. Serve with sliced cucumber.

Caviar

Caviar is a shocking price. Danish lumpfish roe is much cheaper than caviar but gives a similar, rather splendid effect. Serve with chopped egg white.

Elizabeth Baekland
Summer Dish

Consommé   *Sour cream*
Mock caviar (Danish lumpfish roe)

Glass bowls are vital for this recipe. Put into them a layer of sour cream. Add a layer of caviar and yet another layer of sour cream. Cover the layers with consommé (which has already nearly set in the fridge) and chill until the mixture sets. The different-coloured layers gleam through the glass of the bowls and look very pretty.

- The purest and most thoughtful minds are those which love colour the most.

  John Ruskin (1819–1900)
  The Stones of Venice

Kippers, Scandinavian-style

First-class kipper fillets can be marinated in lemon juice and served instead of smoked salmon with brown bread and butter.

Blinis

Serves 4

Pancakes
1 pint milk
4 oz buckwheat flour   Nutmeg
1 egg   Pinch of salt

Filling
8 oz red caviar, or   8 oz smoked trout, and
8 oz smoked salmon, or   ½ pint sour cream

Blend/mix the pancake ingredients together well. Cook in lightly oiled pan until set and lightly browned. Fill pancakes with sour cream and one of the above fillings, serve with ½ lemon per person. Sprinkle with cress.

If you make the pancakes in advance then warm them in the oven, this is very little trouble but gives an amazing impression.

Noële Gordon
Detmolderhof Cocktail

Serves 4

1 tin artichoke hearts
2 jars quails' eggs
8 oz prawns – frozen or tinned
French vinaigrette dressing

1 jar caviar-style lumpfish roe,
or anchovy fillets and olives

Open tin and jars. Arrange three or four artichoke hearts in each of four individual dishes (glass or crystal are best). Drain eggs and place one egg on each artichoke heart. Sprinkle 2 oz prawns (drained or thawed) over each portion. Spoon over vinaigrette dressing and garnish with caviar-style lumpfish roe. Serve chilled with brown bread and butter or crusty French bread, according to taste. Anchovy fillets and olives make an alternative garnish if preferred.

● *Par délicatesse j'ai perdu ma vie.*
Arthur Rimbaud (1854–91)

Professor Glyn Daniel
Scrambled Eggs and Shrimps

Serves 2

Butter for scrambling
4 eggs
2 oz tinned or defrosted frozen shrimps

Salt and pepper
A little grated cheese (optional)

If shrimps are tinned, drain carefully. Then warm them through in butter and keep warm. Season the eggs and scramble them. Fold in the shrimps. Serve on toast or with toast on the side. A little grated cheese may be sprinkled on the egg mixture.

Anchovy Roll

Frozen puff pastry (or roll-once recipe, see below)
Anchovies, flattened between two sheets of greaseproof paper with a rolling pin

Place anchovies on the thawed and rolled puff pastry. Form into a roll. Cut it into slices and place in hot oven. Eat when the pastry is cooked, risen and lightly browned.

For roll-once puff pastry take 8 oz flour, 8 oz salted butter and soda water. Sift the flour into a chilled bowl and grate the butter (straight from the freezer) into it. Mix with just enough chilled soda water to hold it together. Roll out and use at once, or freeze until needed.

"My aunt had a recipe for anchovy essence & tapioca — she called it caviar"

Smoked Mackerel Pâté*

1 smoked mackerel	A little grated onion
4 oz cottage or cream cheese	Fresh lemon juice

Blend or mash all ingredients, starting with the skinned and boned mackerel and adding the rest gradually.

You can substitute poached kipper fillets for the smoked mackerel, and then you have Kipper Pâté.

Mrs Seamus Heaney
Tuna Pâté*

1 × 7 oz can tuna fish	Salt and pepper
A lot of butter (about $\frac{1}{4}$ lb – Eds)	Squeeze of lemon

Blend or mash ingredients together with a fork. Chill. Serve with toast. A squeeze of lemon sharpens the flavour.

Cod's Roe Pâté (Taramasalata)*

1 thin slice of white bread, soaked in water and squeezed dry
4 oz jar smoked cod's roe (or $\frac{1}{4}$ lb piece)
1 small boiled potato (use extra bread if you have no potato handy)

1 cup oil	1 clove garlic
Juice of $\frac{1}{2}$ lemon	Salt and pepper
Parsley	

Blend all ingredients except the oil until they are well mixed. Pour in oil gradually until it is assimilated. Serve the pâté with chives, cucumber and toast.

* It is difficult to say how many people these pâtés will serve. It has been remarked that eating pâté and toast is rather like playing ping-pong – one hardly knows when to stop – but on the whole, the quantities given here will serve 4–6 people.

Ursula Vaughan Williams
Sardines

These are much nicer hot than cold. Open the tin, drain the oil into a small frying pan and let it get very hot. Fry the sardines briskly until they are crisp and brown on both sides. Drain for a few seconds on kitchen paper, and eat them at once, preferably with a squeeze of lemon, and if possible, brown bread and butter.

This dish is also useful for people who want a meal suddenly and are bored with it always having to be scrambled eggs. It takes 5 minutes – if you can get the tin open easily.

Harrods keep very posh sardines that have matured in the tin, and many foreign brands are better than British, especially Spanish and Portuguese. (Eds)

- A man is in general better pleased when he has a good dinner upon his table than when his wife talks Greek. My old friend, Mrs Carter, could make a pudding as well as translate Epictetus.

    James Boswell (1740–95)
    Life of Samuel Johnson

Jellied Eels

You must buy live eels and get the fishmonger to cut off their heads. Wash them very thoroughly and cut them into inch-long sections. Put in a pan and barely cover with water. Season and simmer for about 15 minutes or until the eels are tender. Pour the contents of the pan into a dish and leave in a cool place to set.

Traditionally, Londoners eat them either cold and jellied with vinegar, or hot with mash and 'liquor', which is a white sauce made with the cooking liquid and parsley. One foot-long eel will serve 2–3 people.

If you serve them as a first course, arrange them on a bed of lettuce and garnish with onion rings and tomatoes.

If cooking them yourself seems too much trouble, buy them ready jellied from a delicatessen.

- While the angels, all pallid and wan,
  Uprising, unveiling, affirm
  That the play is the tragedy, 'Man'
  And its hero the Conqueror Worm.

> Edgar Allan Poe (1809–49)
> *The Conqueror Worm*

Fay Maschler
Shrimps Sautéed with Garlic

Serves 4–6

1 lb small brown shrimps (the kind you can, and should, eat in their entirety)
2 or 3 fat cloves garlic
Olive oil
Cayenne pepper
French bread for mopping

Chop the peeled cloves of garlic very finely. If you smash them through a garlic press, they burn too quickly. Cover the bottom of a shallow copper sauté pan or frying pan with oil. Heat to medium hot. Add the garlic, stir around for a moment, and add the shrimps. Turn up the heat and cook the shrimps briefly but fiercely, turning them about with a wooden fork or spoon. Sprinkle with cayenne pepper. Serve whilst they are sizzling, with bread to soak up the shrimpy, garlicky oil.

"You are going to eat in tonight"

**Mrs Eileen Byrne,
who has cooked professionally for 15 years**

Salmon Mousse

Serves 6

2 × 7 oz cans pink salmon
3 tablespoons Hellman's mayonnaise
1 cube Knorr chicken stock
2 tablespoons double cream
1 sachet gelatine
1 egg white
Cucumber for garnish

Mash salmon into mayonnaise. Dilute chicken cube with a tablespoon of boiling water and juice from the can and add gelatine and cream. When the gelatine has completely melted, mix all together. Whisk an egg white and fold it in. Put in the fridge to set.

I always use the juice of the salmon, which gives this mousse such a good taste. If you have a salmon mould, it looks a bit special. The mousse must be served on a lovely dish with lots of cucumber. It's one of the most delicious things I've ever eaten in my life.

Mrs Eileen Byrne
Yoghourt Mousse

Serves 4

1 can consommé (Crosse & Blackwell)
1 small carton natural yoghourt
1 clove crushed garlic
A pinch of paprika or cayenne pepper
Black olives for garnish

Blend or whip all ingredients and leave in the fridge to set.

    Serve this to people who are obsessed with counting their calories. Its calorie count couldn't be lower, but it looks quite rich and creamy. One mustn't forget to sprinkle a very generous pinch of paprika – or a little less cayenne pepper – over the mousse. The brilliant colour of the paprika brightens up all that 'beige', and black olives are perfect with it.

Zita Mulhern
Magimix Chicken Liver Pâté

Serves 4–6

1 lb chicken livers
2 tablespoons chopped onion
5 oz butter
1 clove of garlic (optional)
2 fl oz sherry or brandy
1 fl oz cream
$\frac{1}{2}$ teaspoon salt
$\frac{1}{8}$ teaspoon pepper
$\frac{1}{8}$ teaspoon mixed spice
1 pinch of thyme

Melt 1 oz of the butter in pan. Fry onions, and then livers, having removed any greenish spots, until just stiffened but still rosy inside. Scrape into Magimix bowl. Pour sherry or brandy into pan and reduce to 3 tablespoons. Scrape into Magimix bowl. Melt remaining 4 oz butter and pour into Magimix bowl, adding all the remaining ingredients. Process with metal blade until the pâté is very smooth. Check seasoning and pour into mould or individual ramekins. A further 2 oz melted butter may be floated on top to seal flavour if desired.

Potted Chicken

Cooked chicken can be pounded, or blended with a clove of garlic, a pinch of fresh tarragon or some lemon zest, and either cream cheese or butter to give a smooth consistency. A little left-over ham can be added if you have some. Left-over roast beef can also be treated in this way and becomes Potted Beef.

David Mlinaric
Anchovy Eggs

Hard-boiled eggs   Anchovies

Halve the eggs, take out the yolks and mash the anchovies into them. Take more anchovies than you can possibly imagine.
  Serve with sliced tomatoes on wholemeal bread with fresh basil on top. This makes a change from more elaborate dishes, as you can taste the pure flavour of the ingredients.

● Un oeuf is as good as a feast.
Hilaire Belloc (1870–1953)

Willie Landels,
***Harpers & Queen* magazine**
Queen's Shape

Serves 4–6

6 hard-boiled eggs
1 teaspoon anchovy paste
1 tablespoon gelatine, melted in
   1 tablespoon hot water
¼ pint whipped cream
Pinch of curry

Salt and pepper
Nutmeg
Prawns or tuna fish
Mayonnaise or
   bunch of watercress

Mince the hard-boiled eggs and mix with anchovy paste, whipped cream and gelatine, pinch of curry, salt, pepper and nutmeg. Pour into a ring mould and leave for half an hour in refrigerator. Take out and turn on to a plate, fill the centre with prawns and mayonnaise, or tuna fish, or a bunch of watercress.

Oeufs en Geleé

Serves 4

4 poached eggs *Chopped tarragon*
Chilled consommé (Crosse & Blackwell) mixed with a little dry sherry

Bring an inch of salted water to the boil in a frying pan. (If you use a saucepan, the eggs vanish into a foaming cloud of egg white. Once they become invisible, they tend to break as one lifts them out.) Drop in the eggs from a cup. When they set, lift them out with a fish slice rather than a poaching spoon. Let the water drip off. Place each egg in a ramekin and let cool. Cover with chilled consommé. Sprinkle with lots of chopped tarragon. Serve cold. The eggs can, of course, be cooked in a poaching device, but then they acquire an unpleasant rubbery texture.

● I expect that Woman will be the last thing civilized by Man.
George Meredith (1828–1909)
The Ordeal of Richard Feverel

Chicory and Egg Salad

Serves 4

1 lb chicory *Mayonnaise (Hellman's)*
2 hard-boiled eggs (chopped) *Chives or spring onions*

Cut chicory sticks into thick rings. Mix up with eggs and mayonnaise. Sprinkle with chopped chives or spring onions.

The crisp texture of the chicory together with the rich mayonnaise makes this hors d'oeuvre, but mix it all up at the last moment, otherwise the chicory will get soggy.

The best way to eat avocados is without dressing

Avocado Par Excellence

The best way to eat avocados is without dressing.

Unripe avocados can be placed on the radiator to speed their ripening. They must never be left frying there for too long however; otherwise they turn a frighteningly funereal shade.

Perfect avocados
Lemon and rock salt

Cut avocados in half and remove stones. Serve with lemon and salt. If they are perfect, they need nothing else.

Avocados Caroline

Serves 4

2 avocados	*1 tablespoon vinegar*
2 hard-boiled eggs	*2 crushed cloves of garlic*
1 tomato	*4 or 5 chopped spring onions*
3 tablespoons olive oil	

This recipe is recommended for avocados that have been forgotten and allowed to cook in their skin on the radiator – for avocados that have become slushy, dark and over-ripe.

Scoop out all the murky flesh from some unprepossessing avocados. Mash it in a bowl or blend with the hard-boiled eggs and crushed garlic. Make a dressing with the oil and vinegar. Season, and add the pulp of a tomato. Pour the dressing over the mixture and add chopped spring onions to it, so that it regains a pleasant green shade. Serve with rock salt and toast. This dish is very filling because of the eggs and can therefore be given as a main course to children.

**Mrs T. Rochon,
Chez Solange Restaurant**

Avocado Chez Solange

Serves 4

2 avocado pears	*Salt and pepper*
4 spring onions	*4 oz low-fat natural yoghourt*
Juice of a lemon	*4 or 5 button mushrooms*

In a Kenwood blender put the spring onions with the yoghourt and mix until a really fine mixture. Add to this chunks of avocado, lemon juice, salt and pepper and blend again. Pour the mixture into champagne coupes and decorate with slightly steamed, sliced mushrooms. Put in the fridge and serve very chilled.

Toni Harrison Kahn
Baked Avocado

Serves 4

As a minicab driver, keeping odd hours, I have had to work out a number of dishes that are easy to prepare and delicious to eat. Baked avocado is very simple but a bit different.

2 avocados
1 tablespoon onion juice
1 green pepper, chopped
1 tablespoon chopped dill pickle
French dressing
½ tablespoon chopped chives
2 tablespoons chopped parsley

Cut avocados in half as usual, bake in their skins for 15 minutes in a moderate oven with a little oil sprinkled over the flesh. Mix other ingredients together and pour on just before serving.

Neal Street Restaurant
Avocado, Bacon and Lettuce Salad

Crispy lettuce (Iceberg type)
Ripe avocado
Streaky bacon
Vinaigrette

First prepare in an ordinary-size salad bowl, the lettuce and chopped pieces of avocado. Fry a small quantity of streaky bacon and add this to the top of the salad (including what melted fat might be with the bacon); serve immediately while bacon is still hot and add a vinaigrette according to taste.

Peter, Chef at the Popote Restaurant
Popote Stilton Pears

A light and unusual summer starter.
    Take one ripe dessert pear per portion, and some Stilton. Wash pears but do not peel. Decore the pears with an apple corer. Mix the Stilton with a little cream and port until it is the consistency of butter.
    Stuff pears with the above mixture, refrigerate (do not freeze), covering the exposed ends of the pears with foil to prevent discolouration.
    To serve, slice stuffed pears thinly and pour over them a sweetened vinaigrette. Because pears have to be refrigerated, they can be prepared 3 or 4 hours in advance.

Ann Dunn
Instant Aigrettes

Swiss processed cheese   *Eggs*
  (the little wrapped triangles)   *Breadcrumbs*

Dip triangles of Swiss processed cheese in beaten egg and breadcrumbs. Fry quickly in hot oil, and drain. Serve (ideally) with fresh sorrel tossed in a vinaigrette dressing, otherwise cucumber or tomato salad – very oily and garlicky.
    A better dish than it sounds.

Crudités

Wash and separate into tiny florets a crisp cauliflower head. Cut young carrots and a cucumber into sticks, and crisp green and red peppers into rings. Wash young celery in iced water. Add any available suitable vegetables, properly cut, to dip into the mayonnaise – which you have put in a big bowl and to which you have added chopped parsley, mint and any other appropriate herb you can lay hands on. Children enjoy this. Provide coarse salt for anyone eschewing mayonnaise.

Fetta Cheese

Blend fetta with olive oil and garlic and serve with hot pitta bread. Offer tinned stuffed vine leaves, pickled chillies and olives. (You will need to have access to a Cypriot shop.)

Antipasto

Take very thinly sliced ham, salami and any other Italian sausage you can find. Serve on individual plates and adorn with olives, quarters of hard tomato, sliced gherkin, crisp heart of lettuce – almost anything you have to hand. If you are sufficiently generous with this, your second course can be a simple dish – Spaghetti Carbonara (p. 140) or Fish Florentine (p. 101).

Melon and Parma ham

A simple and classic first course. If you can buy fresh figs, serve them instead of the melon.

Jane Conway Gordon
Tomato Ice Cream

Serves 4

2–3 tomatoes, depending on size
Juice of ½ lemon
Tomato ketchup to taste

4 oz double cream, whipped
Salt, pepper

Put tomatoes through a mill or liquidiser, and sieve (to eliminate skin). Add remaining ingredients in given order. Freeze at lowest possible temperature, until firm. Beat at half time (to eliminate crystals).

**Vanessa de Lisle,
Fashion Editor, *Harpers & Queen* magazine**

Parmesan Cheese Ice Cream

Serves 4–6

6 oz ground Parmesan cheese
1 pint double cream
1 teaspoon dry Coleman's mustard
Ground black pepper
Paprika
Plain wafers
A little butter

Pour the double cream into a bowl and mix with the mustard, lots of black pepper and ground Parmesan. Then pour into ice tray and freeze. When ready to serve, melt butter and brush either side of ice cream wafers with it, sprinkle with pepper and salt and brown on a wire tray in oven until golden. Make lots as they are delicious. Slice ice cream on to pretty plate and sprinkle with paprika.

Soups

> I do not want Michelangelo for breakfast – for luncheon – for dinner – for tea – for supper – for between meals.
>
> Mark Twain (1835–1910)
> *Innocents Abroad*

Bread Upon the Waters

Nice crisp croûtons enliven most soups but are a nuisance if you have to fry them at the last minute. Butter slices of bread (garlic butter is good for more robust soups, or anchovy butter with fish soups, p. 156), allowing one slice per person. Pour a tablespoon or two of sunflower oil into a roasting pan, cut the bread into dice and put them, unbuttered side down, in the pan. Crisp them quickly in a hot oven or cook slowly on the bottom until golden.

Fried breadcrumbs can also be cooked in this way – mince fresh bread and cook in the oven mixed into a blend of melted butter and sunflower oil.

Nicholas Haslam
Quick Bisque

Serves 6–8

2 cans lobster or crab meat
1 can turtle soup
1 can condensed tomato soup
1 can pea soup
1 can beef bouillon or consommé
1 teaspoon of dried onions, reconstituted with a very little hot water
1½ cartons cream
Brandy

Heat all the ingredients, adding the cream and brandy at the very end. Served with croûtons, this is a meal in itself.

- Stretched on the rack of a too easy chair.
>
> Alexander Pope (1688–1744)
> *The Dunciad*

Mrs Richard Ryan
Korean Fish Soup

Serves 4

1 lb cod, whiting or eel, sliced
1 pint chicken broth
2 slices of turnip, finely chopped
2 chopped leeks
Soy sauce
Cayenne pepper

Quickly boil up the fish and vegetables in the chicken broth. When they are cooked through, add some soy sauce and cayenne pepper.

This is a very fresh tasting and unusual soup.

Kuniko Kobayashi, actress
Japanese Quick Soup

Serves 1–2

1 egg
1 Knorr cube
Broccoli or other green vegetable
Dried seaweed
Tongarashi – a Japanese form of pepper available from Oriental supermarkets

Melt the Knorr cube in enough water to taste. Add the dried seaweed, with Japanese pepper and the green vegetable. When the mixture becomes a boiling soup, throw in any herbs you happen to have. Stir in the raw egg and serve.

Crab Soup

Serves 4–6

1 small onion
A little butter
1 × ½ lb packet frozen crab
1 pint chicken cube stock
1 tablespoon tomato purée
1 glass sherry
Cream or yoghourt
Cayenne pepper or paprika

Melt an onion in some butter. Add the frozen crab and stir until it melts. Add the chicken cube stock and tomato purée. Boil for one minute. Remove from heat, add sherry and taste for seasoning. Add a few spoonfuls of cream or yoghourt and serve, sprinkled with cayenne or paprika.

I know its à la mode, darling, but.... de quoi?

Drones Restaurant
Avocado Prawn Soup

Serves 6–8

4 avocados
2½ pints milk
Salt and pepper
4 oz peeled prawns
Cayenne pepper

Peel and stone the avocados. Put avocados and milk in blender and blend until creamy. Season to taste. Chill, serve in consommé cups or soup bowls. Drop whole peeled prawns on top of soup. Sprinkle with cayenne pepper. Serve.

Ann Dunn
A Quick Fish Soup

Serves 4

1 fish head
Onion
Bouquet garni
1 × 7 oz tin tuna fish
4 cloves of garlic
A pinch of saffron
1½ pints water

Boil vigorously a fish head with onion and bouquet garni in a saucepan of water. Put resulting bouillon in a mixer with a can of tuna fish in oil and 4 cloves of garlic. Mix at high speed into a rough cream. Reheat and add saffron. Serve with croûtons and grated cheese.

Xandra Hardie
Almond Soup

Serves 4

An incredibly quick, easy cold soup, but give it half an hour in the fridge to chill.

1 large carton plain yoghourt
2 oz packet skinned almonds
2 cloves of garlic
4 tablespoons olive oil
Lemon juice, salt, pepper, as you like
White grapes, peeled and seeded (optional)

Put it all in a liquidiser until the almonds are ground up. It has a lovely smooth taste with a sharp edge. If you have time, or a slave, add peeled and seeded white grapes before serving.

Lucian Freud
Tomato Soup au Naturel

Fresh tomatoes *Clotted cream*
Country butter *Bay leaf*

My recipe is not right for this book. I once took only the very purest ingredients. I first fried the tomatoes very slowly. I then simmered them very slowly, stirring all the time. The whole thing took hours. When I tasted it I realised I had re-invented Heinz Tomato Soup.

**Mrs Myrtle Allen,
Ballymaloe Restaurant, Shanagarry, Co. Cork,
(and author of *The Ballymaloe Cookbook*)**
Brussels Sprout Soup

Serves 3–4

2 cups frozen sprouts   *Salt and pepper*
Light stock or chicken bouillon *1 tablespoon cream (optional)*

Barely cover the sprouts in water and boil them fast, turning them occasionally in an uncovered pan until they are soft. Liquidise or sieve them. Thin out with stock to desired consistency. Add salt and pepper, and perhaps a little cream.

You can use spinach, lettuce or sorrel instead. (Eds)

Kieran Tunney
Potato Soup

Serves 6

6–8 potatoes
1 lb onions
6 cloves of garlic
Water, milk
Seasoning

This was Tallulah Bankhead's favourite soup. It cures colds. It cures anything. Maybe I should be more precise – let's say that this soup *halves* your cold.

Chop all the vegetables, boil until soft and falling apart. Add milk. Season and reheat.

Another

Grind up 3 or 4 cloves of garlic. Make up a large packet of instant potato. Put it in a pan with the garlic, a chicken stock cube and enough milk or milk and water to make thick soup consistency. Heat through and serve with croûtons.

Quick Thick Lentil Soup

Serves 6–8

*1 lb packet Whitworth's
  orange lentils
Onion (dried or fresh)
Any left-over vegetables,
  or a handful of frozen mixed
Any left-over sausage,
  bits of bacon, or pork
  chopped up
Water or stock to cover
  (watch out for
  evaporation)*

Season and cook. Watch out for foaming over – reduce heat once it has come to the boil and simmer until thick: 10–15 minutes.

Served with hot garlic bread, this should either follow or precede a cold course. It is very filling, and has a countrified, home-is-the-hunter, air about it.

Ursula Vaughan Williams
Yvonne's Washing-Day Soup

Serves 4

Yvonne came from Guernsey; her mother used to make this soup for the farm workers on Mondays.

1 lb onions (large ones if possible, as they are quicker to chop)	2 pints milk (or half milk, half water, or white stock)
2 oz butter	
2 oz flour	Salt, black pepper

Melt the butter in a deep saucepan while you peel and chop the onions. Put the onions into the butter when it is foaming a little, and stir them well until they are colouring. Add the flour, then the liquid, stirring all the time, until the soup thickens and comes to the boil. Taste and season. Remove from heat and serve from the saucepan.

It is advisable to make enough for second, and probably third helpings.

If you can make toasted cheese under the grill while you are making the soup, this provides a splendid lunch in about 15 minutes.

Connie Strigner
Another

The French make a gorgeous soup with onions, eggs and fried bread. Fry the onions until soft, which takes about ten minutes, then add either water, milk or chicken stock – a cube will do.

When it is boiling drop in raw eggs and stir, and pour over thick slices of fried bread. Grated cheese can be sprinkled on top if you like.

Watercress Soup

Serves 4

1 cup made-up instant potato
1 bunch watercress
2 chicken stock cubes
2 egg yolks
2 pints water

Melt the cubes in the hot water, gradually stir in the potato, add the watercress and boil for one minute. Blend and reheat. Stir a little of the soup into the yolks. Remove soup from heat and gradually add the yolk mixture. Serve at once.

'Lucrezia'
Soupe Mauvaise Femme

Serves 4–6

1 oz dried onions
1 large packet Smash
1 can carrots
2 pints water, approximately
3 oz butter
Salt and black pepper
Butter

Soak onions in hot water for 10 minutes. Drain the carrots, add to the water and onions in the pan. Simmer for 5 minutes. Slowly add the Smash, stirring all the time. Whizz in a blender or food processor with butter and salt until smooth. Reheat, add more water if required. Serve with knobs of butter in each bowl.

Borscht

Serves 4–6

2 medium-sized, already-boiled beetroots
1 packet dried mixed vegetables
1 beef stock cube

Sour cream or yoghourt
2 pints water

Prepare the stock cube with a pint and a half of boiling water and simmer the vegetables in it until they soften. Liquidise one beetroot and shred the other. Add to the vegetables. Heat well. Then add your cream or yoghourt.

Hot Cucumber Soup with Dill

Serves 4

½ an unpeeled cucumber
1 onion
1 pint chicken stock

Cream
Lemon juice
Fresh or bottled dill

Cut up half an unpeeled cucumber and an onion and cook in about a pint of chicken stock (Knorr cube). When soft, liquidise, add cream, seasoning and a little lemon juice. The chopped dill on top makes this cucumber soup exquisite and is the easiest herb to grow in your garden or window box. Unlike other herbs that need care and attention and often get lost in the garden because of the lack of it, dill grows into a bushy kind of weed that towers even over your uncut grass.

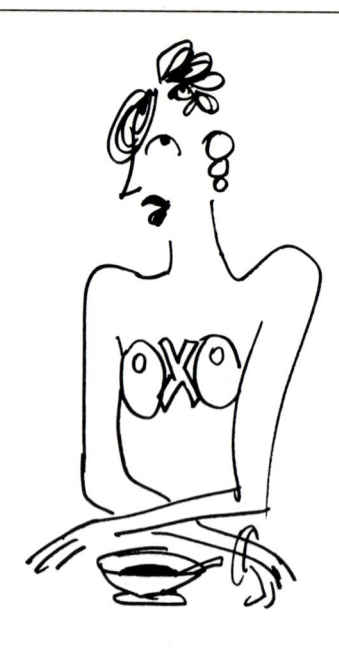

86 *Darling, you shouldn't have gone to so much trouble*

"I've got the recipe tucked away somewhere"

Cold Cucumber Soup

Serves 4

- 2 cucumbers
- 2 cloves of garlic
- 3 tablespoons olive oil
- 1 tablespoon vinegar
- Chopped onion
- ½ pint water
- Salt

Put all ingredients into a blender and then chill. Serve very cold. Add cream or yoghourt to bowls.

Philippa Davenport
Iced Tomato Soup with Basil

Serves 6

½ *pint soured cream*
1 clove of garlic
2 teaspoons lemon juice
1 teaspoon caster sugar

2 × 14 oz cans Italian tomatoes
Fresh basil
Salt, black pepper

Crush a garlic clove (a smallish one) with some salt. Put it into a liquidiser together with a small handful of fresh basil leaves. Add 2 teaspoons lemon juice, 1 teaspoon caster sugar, a good grinding of black pepper and ¼ pint soured cream. Blend until reduced to a smooth purée. Add the contents of two 14 oz cans of Italian tomatoes and blend again. Finally, blend in another ¼ pint soured cream, taste and add extra lemon, garlic, pepper, sugar and salt if wished – bearing in mind that the garlic flavour will become more pronounced while the soup stands. Cover and refrigerate until icy cold (if the canned tomatoes and soured cream were refrigerated for several hours before making the soup, chilling will not take long). Serve garnished with a little extra fresh chopped basil or wafer thin slices of cucumber.

Another, with Dill

A delicious variation of this soup encountered in New York is made out of fresh tomatoes, garlic, salt, pepper and chicken stock with fresh orange juice added to taste (up to equal quantities). We tried it with tinned tomatoes and bottled orange juice and it worked just as well. Float fresh dill on top if you have some. Equally good hot or cold. (Eds)

Stanley's Gazpacho

Serves 4

1½ cans Campbell's tomato soup
1 cup V-8 vegetable juice
Garlic
1 large mild onion, chopped
1 cucumber, chopped
2 green peppers, chopped

Add to the tomato soup one cup of V-8, and garlic, chopped onion, chopped cucumber and chopped green peppers. Anything else in the house that is green. No need to blend.

Sue MacGregor
Cheat's Pea Soup

Here's a *very* quick soup recipe which you may think too boring for words: but it *is* quick and quite a pretty colour.

Serves 4

1 medium packet frozen peas
1 pint chicken stock
Mint
Sour cream

Cook peas in well seasoned chicken stock. Put this and 6–10 mint leaves into liquidiser and whizz up. The soup will be fairly thick. Serve hot or cold with a blob of sour cream on top and, if you like, a sprinkling of chopped mint too.
This is not at all boring but very good. (Eds)

Elizabeth Baekland
Chicken Soup

Serves 6

Small pieces of cooked chicken
1 can mushroom soup
1 can creamed chicken soup
Mushrooms
Red wine

Heat the canned soups and add fresh sliced mushrooms and red wine. The fresh mushrooms are essential. Cook until they are tender. Add the cooked chicken last and heat through.

Bertorelli Bros. Restaurant
Stracciatella Soup

Serves 4–6

2 eggs	Chopped parsley
1 tablespoon grated Parmesan cheese	Seasoning to taste
2 pints chicken broth	

Beat with a fork the eggs, cheese, parsley and a little of the stock. Meanwhile heat the remaining stock and when it comes almost to the boil, pour in the beaten mixture, stirring continuously, and bring just to the boil. Then transfer to a warmed tureen and serve immediately.

Sue Parkin Moore
Summer Soup

Serves 4–6

2 tins Sainsbury's consommé	Walnuts or chives
2 oz Philadelphia cheese	

Use 1½ tins of consommé to half fill glasses or small bowls. Chill in the fridge until jellied. Put the other half tin of soup in the liquidiser with the cheese until mixed. Then pour on top of the jelly. Sprinkle with walnuts or chives.

Chilling time 6 hours, preparation time 3 minutes. A pleasing, Guinness-like effect.

The Countess of Granville
Caviar Soup

Serves 2

1 can Crosse & Blackwell Vichyssoise
1 small glass jar Danish caviar
 (lumpfish roe)
Milk for diluting

Pour a can of pre-chilled Crosse & Blackwell's Vichyssoise into a bowl. Stir the black Danish caviar into the Vichyssoise, which is lumpy and needs to be diluted with cold milk. Avoid using any cream, because this soup is extremely rich and filling. Serve cold, preferably in pretty soup plates. If your guests think you have used real caviar and become embarrassed and say that you shouldn't have done it, smile modestly – but never disillusion them.

This soup is also extremely popular with children and makes a very easy and nourishing main course for lunch or supper.

Rex Cowan
Lokchen Soup

This is chicken soup containing egg vermicelli (*lokchen*). It has to be *lokchen* – no other pasta will do. To those who have eaten it every Friday night as long as they can remember, it is known as Jewish penicillin. At the first sign of illness, despair or assimilation a jar is despatched from the parent household (too much is always made on Thursdays because there can never be enough), and even gentiles are eventually won over by the plain fact that it is the best chicken broth there is. I sometimes have been obliged to take over the role of Jewish mother in our household. I have simplified my mother's recipe a bit, and we eat it as a main course, with no side dishes except one for the bones.

Say oy-veh!

You buy a large boiling fowl from a kosher butcher and he will give you the giblets and the feet, plus the unborn eggs. You scald the chicken in boiling water which makes it easier to remove quills. You put the chicken in a large pan of cold water, together with the giblets, feet, half a large swede, one turnip, 2 onions, 4 carrots, a leek, a stick of celery, all cut into generous chunks, and add salt. No herbs or spices. When it boils, you remove first the scum, and then, for keeping, the chicken fat as it rises to the surface. This takes about half an hour. Then you jam on the lid and leave it to simmer – 3 hours apart from cooking the *lokchen* (separately always). Pop in the eggs 5 minutes before serving. The *lokchen*, drained and cold, are put in each large bowl, to be covered with soup, vegetables and large pieces of chicken.

Quentin Crisp
Tibetan Workhouse Soup

I have never cooked seriously either for myself or for anyone else. In the days when I was too poor to eat in restaurants and was besieged by acquaintances even nearer to starvation than I, the most I ever did was to take a saucepan which had been used for a variety of purposes without ever being washed, fill it with water and bring it to the boil. The result was known as Workhouse Soup. As, naturally, very little of this brew was consumed, on subsequent occasions I added to it anything that came to hand. The more 'acquired' (nasty) the flavour became, the more distant the places in which I said the recipe had originated. When a consistency of cake and a state of uneatability was reached, I described the dish as Tibetan.

Working on this principle you do not need a great many recipes – just a large number of friends.

It's the Tibetan national dish – called Yuk.

Fish

The dame of a man of independence should be proud of her position; she should try and remedy the evil that drives her husband to his club. If ... she be unable to read a cookery book let her employ some one above the woman she employs to clean her street door step – a woman born in a shed, or under the lee of a brick kiln, who most probably never tasted meat in the hole from whence she came. Common sense dictates that such a person ought not to be entrusted to cook anything beyond what is fitted for the pigsty.

Anon. (19th century)

**M. Jacques Viney, F.C.F.A., A.C.F.,
Chevalier du Mérite Agricole, Maîtres-Cuisiniers,
Craft Guild of Chefs, Chef at the Ritz**

Coquilles des Fruits de Mer Parisiennes

Serves 4

2 oz butter	Garlic
2 large scallops	1 egg yolk
4 oz cod or fresh haddock	1 cup sliced mushrooms (white)
4 oz scampi	½ cup cream
2 oz prawns	½ cup white wine (dry)
1 shallot or ½ onion	2 tablespoons cognac
Chopped parsley	1 tablespoon sherry
Salt, pepper	2 oz grated Parmesan
Fresh tomato concentrate (optional)	8 small scallop shells

Put 2 oz butter in pan, then shallot or onion, chopped fine. Add the scallops, scampi, prawns, cod or fresh haddock, cut into dice. Then add sliced mushrooms. Cook gently. Then pour in the cognac set alight; then the sherry and white wine. Simmer until the juice of the seafood and liquor is reduced by half. Add the cream and simmer once more on low fire, but do not boil. Season and taste. When liquid starts to thicken, take pan off the fire. Add the yolk of egg, well beaten. Keep stirring until nice and creamy. Add chopped parsley. Taste again. If it needs more seasoning a little fresh tomato concentrate can be added, and a soupçon of garlic. Fill each shell to the brim. Sprinkle a little Parmesan on each. Lay the shells on a bed of salt; that way they will keep straight. Then brown in a hot oven or under grill for ten minutes. Then serve piping hot.

A green salad on a side plate can be served (lemon dressing).

For a good wine to drink with this excellent dish, take a Puligny-Montrachet 1970 or a Pouilly-Fuissé 1972, both to be very cold, not chilled.

We were astonished to learn that this recipe only took 15 minutes once the requisite slicing was done. (Eds)

- *Fais énergiquement ta longue et lourde tâche.*
  Puis, après, comme moi, souffres et meurs sans parler.
  Alfred de Vigny (1797–1863)

Barbara Cartland
(cooked by her chef Nigel Gordon in 10 minutes)
Crabmeat à la King

Serves 4

1½ lb crabmeat (white meat only)
2 oz butter
2 oz diced pimento
¾ pint double cream
Seasoning

Melt a little butter in a saucepan, add the crabmeat and heat through. Pour on the cream, bring to the boil, add the diced pimento, season and simmer for 2 minutes. Serve in a round porcelain dish and evenly cover with Sabayon (see below). Then decorate with strips of pimento in the shape of a K.

Serve with Riz pilaff or plain boiled rice.

Sabayon

2 egg yolks   2 tots of brandy

Whisk these two together over a very low heat until they become light and frothy. If the heat is too strong the yolks will scramble.

Nigel Gordon: If you live in the country then you should order your crabmeat a few days before you want it, as crab that has been in the deep freeze tends to lose its flavour.

Barbara Cartland: A book called *Le tableau de la vie conjugale*, which was published in France in 1696, was written by a doctor. He promised that 'old men will learn how to behave with a young wife so as to be able to procreate children and become stimulated without any damage to their health'. The foods the doctor thought sexually exciting were – the yolks of eggs, testicles of cocks, the marrow of beef, crabs, shrimps, milk, artichokes, garlic and skink.

- Who is she that looketh forth in the morning, fair as the moon, clear as the sun and terrible as an army with banners?

    The Song of Solomon

Barbara Cartland
(cooked by her chef Nigel Gordon in 10 minutes)
Filets de Sole Caprice

2 pieces of fillet of sole per person	Milk
1 banana per person	Flour
1 tablespoon chutney	Olive oil and butter
4 oz butter	

Dip the fillets of sole in milk, then in flour. Also the banana. Fry them in a 50–50 mixture of olive oil and butter until golden brown. Season with salt and pepper.

Place the fillets of sole on a serving dish with bananas on top. Add a little fried butter over them and garnish with chutney.

Nigel Gordon: If you wish to keep to health foods use vegetable margarine instead of butter, and mango or apple chutney.

Barbara Cartland: The banana is so sustaining that three dozen will keep a man alive for a week. Bananas contain a large amount of carbohydrates, potassium, magnesium and phosphorous, besides calcium, iron and sulphur. The ripe fruit is rich in vitamins. Owing to its shape it has been used in black magic ceremonies. There is an Apache love chant which says:

>   Eat the banana.
>   I look at him.
>   I give him the banana.
>   As the banana is with the man,
>   So will the man be with me.

Bill Staughton,
(chef at the Hungry Horse Restaurant)
Hungry Horse Kedgeree

*Smoked Finnan haddock
  or Scotch salmon
Long grain rice (Patna type)
Onion
Red and green pimentos
Cayenne pepper
Turmeric powder
Fresh cream
Chopped parsley
Hard-boiled eggs
Butter
Salt*

The fish of your choice must be poached first, and after cooking, flaked and boned. Cook the rice with salt until *al dente*, turn out into a colander, wash well with cold water and allow to drain until dry.

Chop the onion finely, also the pimentos. Melt the butter in a heavy frying pan then add the chopped onion and pimentos, add salt, cayenne pepper and turmeric. When the onion and pimentos are soft, but not browned, add the flaked fish and cook together. When they are heated add the cold rice and stir until the whole mixture is well heated. Take off the heat and put the kedgeree into an oven-proof dish and leave until it is needed at a later date.

To finish, put this mixture into the oven and heat through under silver foil until it is thoroughly hot, perhaps adding a little more butter. Then add the cream and stir into the kedgeree, using enough only to moisten. The reheating process should take about 20–30 minutes.

At this point the kedgeree is ready for the table but before serving, sprinkle the chopped parsley and hard-boiled eggs over it as a garnish.

Magnus Pyke
Another

Serves 2

4 oz rice	2 oz butter
1 Finnan haddock	Cayenne pepper
2 eggs	

This recipe for kedgeree is not particularly original but it is popular nevertheless.

Put 4 oz rice on to boil for 16 minutes; meanwhile boil a Finnan haddock in a frying pan; and hard-boil two eggs. Fish out the haddock and while dissecting off the flesh let 2 oz butter melt in frying pan; mix the scrunched-up fish with it; add the drained and washed rice. While all this is going on, the eggs have been cooling under the cold tap. Add one chopped egg, and mix the whole lot with as much cayenne pepper as you can stand. Pile the mix into a dish and put slices of hard-boiled egg all over it.

Lovely.

Another, with Sardines

Use tinned sardines instead of fresh fish, adding the oil from the tin instead of butter. English people in India often preferred to use tinned sardines rather than fresh fish as they could never be sure where the fish had been.

Louise Bootes-Johns,
Harpers & Queen **magazine**
Willie's Prawns

Serves 3

1 lb frozen peeled prawns	Worcestershire sauce
½ pint single cream	½ lb mushrooms
Heinz tomato sauce	1 cup of rice

Boil the rice and peel the mushrooms. Fry the mushrooms gently in butter – don't over brown them. Drain off grease, then add mushrooms and prawns (washed) to the following mixture: tomato sauce, to taste, with cream, stirred well, and Worcestershire sauce, to achieve 'prawn cocktail dressing' taste. Put whole lot into a saucepan, and cook very gently (or the cream and tomato sauce will separate) until the prawns are heated through and hot enough to eat. Serve on rice with parsley and something like broccoli.

Very quick instant dinner course if caught out.

Julian Lloyd
Captain's Haddock

Serves 4

Frozen vol-au-vent cases　　*3 eggs*
½ lb smoked haddock　　*Butter*

Fill the cases with scrambled egg and bits of haddock which have been soaking in lemon juice all night and have been well drained, or with a good kipper similarly treated. Heat the cases and serve. An excellent main course for lunch or for an hors d'oeuvre at dinner.

Janet Boud
Fish Florentine

Serves 4

1 lb frozen cod or haddock　　*Cheese sauce*
1 lb frozen leaf spinach

Fry or gently poach the fish. Boil the spinach as instructed on the packet and drain it well. Put the spinach on the bottom of a casserole dish, lay the fish on top and cover with plenty of cheese sauce. Sprinkle with cheese and place in the oven to heat through.

Soused Herring

Have your herrings cleaned and beheaded. Place them side by side in an oven-proof dish, sprinkle with salt and pour over them a mixture of half vinegar (preferably white wine vinegar) and water to reach half-way up their sides. Put two bay leaves on top. Cook, closely covered, in a moderate oven for half an hour. Allow them to cool in the liquor and serve cold with a potato or green salad.

- A whale and a herring were inseparable companions. One day the herring was seen swimming alone. 'Where is the whale?' he was asked. 'Am I my blubber's kipper?' he responded.

Bad joke

Cara Denman
Salmon Bread Soufflé

(The soufflé that doesn't collapse if kept waiting, and can be eaten cold.)

Serves 6

1 lb salmon	3 oz flour
8 oz fresh breadcrumbs	3 eggs
3 oz butter	

Steam the salmon over as little water as possible – be careful not to let the pan boil dry. Reserve the juice and mash the fish. Mix with the breadcrumbs. Make a sauce béchamel by melting 3 oz butter then adding the flour, and stirring continually, gradually add ½ pint of hot milk, salt and pepper, and finally the egg yolks.

Add ¾ of the sauce béchamel to the salmon mixture. Lastly add the stiffly whipped egg whites, folding in lightly and quickly. Butter a savarin tin, fill with the contents and bake in an oven at 375F (mark 5) for 25 minutes.

Meanwhile, make the sauce to cover the soufflé just before serving: combine liquid from steamed salmon, a small quantity of the béchamel, drop of sherry or red wine, lemon juice and a tablespoon of tomato purée. If you use tinned salmon, add 2 tablespoons of tomato purée.

Lobster Salad

Serves 4

1½ cups diced lobster meat or tinned shrimps
½ cup diced celery
2 tablespoons Hellman's mayonnaise
Lettuce

Mix up lobster, celery and mayonnaise. Serve on lettuce.

● *Dis-moi ce que tu manges, je te dirai ce que tu es.*
   Brillat-Savarin (1755–1826)

Shrimps in Cream and Dill

Serves 4

8 tablespoons tinned or frozen shrimps
Enough breadcrumbs to cover shrimps
½ pint single cream
Finely chopped fresh dill
Salt

Butter a shallow dish. Put the shrimps and the chopped dill into it and pour the cream over. Cover thinly with fine breadcrumbs. Add a few tiny knobs of butter and bake in a medium oven for 6 to 10 minutes.

Ailish Marks,
Castletown Restaurant, Celbridge, Co. Kildare
Salmon Steaks Baked in Silver Foil

Salmon steaks *Lemon*
Butter *Parsley butter*
Parsley and chives

Wrap each steak with some butter, parsley and chives in the silver foil, and make a tightly closed, but baggy parcel. Place these parcels in a medium hot oven for about 15 minutes. When cooked, let them stand in a warm place for a few minutes. Serve the steaks with parsley butter and lemon.

Fish in a Dish

Take as many fillets of smoked haddock as you have guests. Gently poach/steam in milk and water, using as little liquid as possible so that it evaporates by the time the fish has cooked. Beat up some eggs (say four eggs to six fillets) in about $\frac{1}{4}$ pint of milk, pour over the fish and cook in a moderate oven until just set. Serve with wholemeal toast and watercress.

Angela Rippon
Fast Fish

Serves 4

4 white fish fillets
1 tablespoon each chopped onion, mushroom, parsley
Butter
2 tablespoons soft white breadcrumbs
1 glass white wine
Seasoning

Fry the onion in half the butter until just soft; add the mushrooms. After one minute add the wine and boil rapidly for another minute. Pour the wine and vegetables over the fillets, which you have placed in a pretty, oven-proof shallow dish. Cover with the breadcrumbs and bits of butter, and cook near the top of the oven 400F (mark 6) for about 15–20 minutes.

- *Vera incessu patuit dea.*
  (The goddess indubitable was revealed in her step.)
  Virgil (70–19 B.C.)
Aeneid, i.

Toni Harrison Kahn
Classic Mackerel

Serves 4

4 mackerel	1 can of gooseberries
1 glass white wine	Sprig of parsley
Fennel seeds	

Clean mackerel, put into baking tin, pour over white wine and put on fennel seeds. Put under grill and cook aproximately 15 minutes either side.

Open can of gooseberries and heat in pan. Put cooked mackerel on plate, drained gooseberries on the side, and pour over juice from baking dish. Add sprig of parsley and serve.

A Scotch method
Cold Salmon

Put your cleaned salmon, or salmon trout, in a fish kettle and cover it with water. Add lemon juice and salt. Cover closely with silver foil and the kettle lid. Bring to the boil and boil for 1 minute, then draw aside. Leave overnight. On no account remove the lid before the following day. Then drain well and serve.

Fish Steaks with Aïoli

Steaks of hake, halibut or turbot *Garlic*
New potatoes *Sea salt*
Mayonnaise

Poach your fish and steam your potatoes. Add to a fine upstanding mayonnaise (you should really make your own for this as it should be the firm wobbly sort that you can cut with a knife, see recipe, p. 151) a great deal of freshly crushed garlic. Resist all temptation to add anything else – it would ruin this meal, which, properly prepared, is one of the world's most superb simple dishes. It is also extremely rich, so begin your meal with a salad and end with a sorbet.

Fresh Trout with Lemon and Butter

(The 'under and over' method which means the fish remains unbroken)

Fresh trout *Butter*
Lemon *Parsley*

Fresh trout does not need any complicated sauces. Be sure to have your fishmonger clean them.

Turn on your grill and let it become blazing hot. Fry the trout in butter in a frying pan on top of the stove. Don't turn the fish, for you will lose a lot of the crispy brown skin. When the trout is fried on one side, put the frying pan under the hot grill and brown the top of the fish. Sprinkle with parsley and lemon.

This is a good method of cooking all small fish or fillets – much easier than trying to turn them.

Fay Maschler
Crab with Ginger and Spring Onion

1 medium-sized crab serves 2

1 crab, preferably uncooked but cooked will do
1 piece ginger root
1 small bunch spring onions

Sauce
2 tablespoons soy sauce
1 heaped teaspoon sugar
1 tablespoon wine vinegar

Clean the crab to the extent of dismembering it and removing the mouth, stomach bag and the bit that looks like creepy little grey fingers from the body. Crack the claws in several places. Peel a piece of ginger root about 1 inch long and take fine slices off it with a vegetable peeler or cut it into julienne strips. Clean the spring onions and slice them lengthwise. Pack the crab pieces into the top of a steamer. Disperse the ginger and spring onions among them. Get the water beneath the steamer boiling heartily and steam the crab until it is hot and the ginger and onions are wilted. Meanwhile, heat together the sauce ingredients until the sugar is melted. A little additional ginger in the sauce is good. Serve the crab with the sauce for dipping. Finger bowls and napkins are called for.

Stanley Moss
Stanley's Fish

White fish fillets – 1 per person
Butter
French mustard
Sour cream
Garlic
Pepper

Smear the fish with the butter and mustard and bake in a moderate oven. Once cooked, add the sour cream, crushed garlic and pepper. Pour the sauce on top of the fish to serve. Allow ½ pint sour cream to six fillets.

Brenda O'Casey
Quick Fish Pie

Serves 6

1–2 lb well washed cod fillet

Marinade
1 cup oil
3 crushed cloves garlic
Handful chopped parsley
Juice of ½ a lemon and zest

Salt and pepper
3 lb boiled potatoes,
* thickly sliced*
Butter

Put the fish in the marinade in the morning.

Arrange potatoes over the top. Dot with butter and cook in hot oven until potatoes are browned and the cod cooked (about ½–¾ hour).

Rex Cowan
Scilly Soup

I sought a rich, hot fish soup to warm the bones of my divers returning from a cold working dive 100 feet below the sea surface. It proved too rare for them but all my other visitors lap it up. I buy from a trawlerman a couple of pounds of megrim or plaice and poach them entire in tin foil, removing only the guts and adding butter and bunches of fennel which grow wild always on sandy shores. We only eat the best bits and throw everything else into a pan of water with a bay leaf, onion and carrot to make stock for the next day.

To make the soup, fry onions and curry together in oil, adding a large tin of tomatoes when done, fennel, a handful of dried green beans, dried onions, pepper and saffron at whim, and simmer. Twenty minutes before serving add slices of potato, pieces of whole fish if you have any, two small squid cut into rings, enough to make the soup a main meal if you want it to be. A few shrimps for fun, not essential, but don't put in any greasy fish like mackerel, herring and sardines, nor anything smoked.

A Respite

Eluned Rowlands
Grapefruit and Noilly Prat Sorbet

Boil in saucepan for 10 minutes ¾ pint of water and 8 oz sugar, until syrupy. Allow to cool.

Add finely grated rind and juice of 2 grapefruit and 2–3 tablespoons of Noilly Prat.

Freeze in a shallow plastic container for 1–2 hours until the mixture has reached a mushy state.

Beat the whites of 2 eggs until stiff.

Turn the frozen mixture into blender. Beat well, and fold in the egg whites.

Freeze again, for the second time, with lid on. Stir once or twice to prevent water from collecting at the bottom of the mixture.

Remove from the freezer 10–15 minutes before serving and serve in frosted glasses.

Eluned Rowlands was a regional winner (Wales) in the *Sunday Times* competition to discover Britain's best cooks. This sorbet is delicious and impressive served between the fish and meat courses, and gives the hostess a welcome breather – to stab the potatoes, add cream to the casserole, etc. (Eds)

Main Courses

> ... take some onions and fry in ghee; cut the green ginger thin; clean the raisins well; take a little ground curry stuff and some tyre; mix all these well together with the meat and boghar the whole thing.
>
> From a recipe for Myhee Kebab,
> *Indian Domestic Economy & Cookery*
> (19th century)

Hot Cold Steak

Rump steak

Marinade
6 chillies (fresh or dried)
3 cloves of garlic
1 tin tomatoes
3 tablespoons oil
1 tablespoon lemon juice
Salt

Blend the marinade ingredients (don't let anyone idly taste a spoonful – it is wickedly hot). Leave the steak in it overnight, turning once or twice. Grill it quickly in the morning – medium rare is better than rare, which might permit the blood to run. In the evening slice it quite thickly and serve cold with hot new potatoes or a tomato or green salad. The marinade can be boiled, cooled and frozen for another time.

Japanese Steak

Steak, finely sliced
Butter
Garlic
Button mushrooms
Tomatoes
Herbs
Soy sauce

Fry steak with all the ingredients, which turn into a sauce.
  This sounds vague but if you use the best steak and finely slice the vegetables it works beautifully. The quantities are entirely a matter of taste and discrimination.

Use a *wok* if you have one, otherwise a heavy iron frying pan. The point of Japanese and Chinese cooking is not to *overcook*. The dish is ready when the steak is as you like it.

Steaks à la Huancaina

Serves 4

4 steaks

Sauce
½ lb cottage cheese *Chopped onion*
2 hard-boiled eggs *Salt and pepper*
Cayenne pepper *Juice of 1 lemon*
¼ pint cream

Liquidise first 3 ingredients for Huancaina sauce, heat and add cream, chopped onion, salt and pepper and lemon juice. Keep warm. Fry steaks and pour sauce over them.

Helen Jones
Steak Tartare

You must know and trust your butcher before you can make this safely. Choose unfrozen fillet steak and ask to see it before getting him to mince it – ideally do it at home in a food processor. Finely chop a Spanish onion – no other nationality will do. Season the steak with freshly ground black pepper and sea salt and mix all together. Serve in soup plates with an unbroken egg yolk on top. Offer Worcestershire sauce. Serve with a green salad.

Keep the egg whites to make meringues, or drink them with Worcestershire sauce the morning after the night before, to line the stomach and still queasiness.

Helen Jones also keeps Welsh mountain sheep, and is very firm about the time they are right to eat – round about the age of twelve months when they are technically 'wethers'. It seems that many are hermaphroditic, but this doesn't matter – their meat is delicious. (Eds)

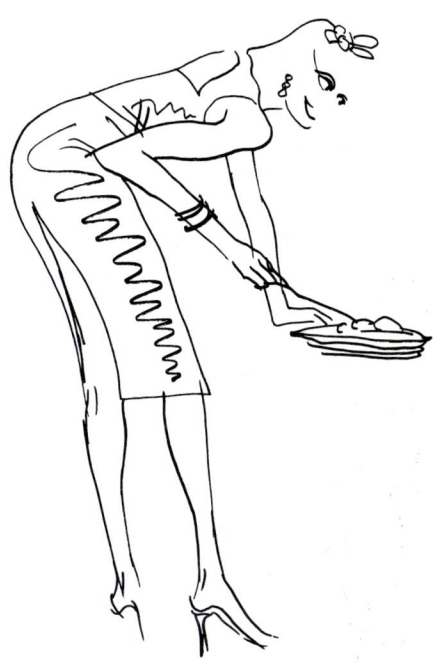

**Myrtle Allen,
Ballymaloe Restaurant**
Beef Cubes

Allow ¼–½ lb steak per person
1 tablespoon white wine
1 teaspoon finely chopped shallots
2 tablespoons stock
1 level teaspoon mixed butter and oil
1 teaspoon butter
½ teaspoon chopped tarragon

Cut meat into ½ inch cubes. Heat butter and oil in a frying pan. Toss the meat in this to required degree, about 4 minutes for medium rare. Remove. Cook shallots in pan for 1 or 2 minutes. Pour in wine and then stock. Cook down to half the quantity. Swirl in herbs and a butter enrichment.

One summer evening I overheard a waitress telling a customer that we had no steaks left. I interrupted the conversation. Yes, we actually had steak meat, but it was all cut into cubes, having been left over from a *fondue bourguignonne* from the previous night. I would sauté the cubes and serve them in a sauce made with the pan juices. Every fortnight or so for some years after this event my customer returned and ordered 'Beef Cubes' for her dinner.

Jane Conway Gordon
Cold Beef or Ham Stroganoff

Serves 6

2 lb fillet of beef (or cooked ham)   1 lb mushrooms

Vinaigrette
6 tablespoons salad oil
2 tablespoons red wine vinegar
1 shallot, finely chopped
1 tablespoon chopped herbs

Sauce
¼ pint sour cream
¼ pint single cream
1 clove of garlic
1 teaspoon paprika
Lemon juice
   or red wine vinegar to taste

Roast fillet with a little oil in a hot oven for about 35 minutes, basting regularly. Allow to cool. Slice mushrooms and cook very quickly for 1 minute in a spoonful of oil. Add paprika and stir. Slice the beef and shred neatly and mix with the mushrooms and vinaigrette dressing.

Crush the garlic with a little salt and mix with the paprika and creams. Season with black pepper and sharpen with vinegar to taste. Pour into a sauce boat and hand with sliced French bread.

Main Courses 117

Sue Gentleman
Boeuf Gentleman

Serves 4

1¼–1½ lb of fillet steak
1 medium onion
4 oz button mushrooms
2 oz unsalted butter
Small carton soured cream

¼ pint good chicken stock
Black pepper
Salt
Parsley

Cut steak into thin strips and chop the onion finely. Melt the butter until it foams, then add the onions and cook for a short time. Add the steak and stir quickly to seal in the juices. Add the whole button mushrooms and stock, and bubble for 4–5 minutes. Finally add the soured cream and seasoning. Reheat, but do not boil. Serve with sprinkled parsley as a garnish and boiled rice or potatoes and a green salad.

Quick Green Stew

Serves 2–3

1 lb of lamb, pork fillet or chicken
Olive oil
3 green tomatoes
3 courgettes
Bunch of spring onions

1 clove of garlic
1 green pepper
10 new potatoes
Bunch of watercress
Carrots or tomatoes

Chop the meat into little cubes. Brown it in the olive oil. Add the next 5 ingredients, chopped, and cover the pan. After 5–10 minutes, when the vegetables have yielded up their juice (keep on a low heat), add the scrubbed potatoes. When they are cooked add the watercress, which you have minced. Very pretty. Serve with nice red carrots or grilled tomatoes.

Pork Chops
with Cadbury's Smash and Cassegrain's Petits Pois

Pork chops
Rashers of smoked bacon
Sprigs of thyme
1 packet of Smash
1 tin of apple purée
1 tin of petits pois

Wrap 2 or 3 rashers of smoked bacon round the trimmed chops and hold them together with toothpicks. This gives the pork a nice smoky flavour. Bake the pork with thyme draped over it in a very hot oven for 20 minutes.

During that time stew some apples or open a tin of apple purée, prepare instant mash and heat up the petits pois.

Rosa Kende,
Co. Kildare
Fillet of Pork in Wine Sauce

Serves 4

1 fillet of pork
Butter
½ lb mushrooms (closed kind)
2 glasses white wine
2 teaspoons tomato purée
Salt and pepper
Parsley

Cut and trim fillet of pork into ½ inch pieces. Heat pan. Fry pieces for 2 minutes each side in butter. Slice mushrooms and sauté in butter in another pan. Add about 2 glasses of white wine and reduce by half. Add 2 teaspoons tomato purée, salt and pepper. Pour over meat and top with parsley.

Sonia Orwell
Pork Chops with Ginger in Orange Juice

Pork chops
Orange juice
Ground or whole ginger
– cut into lumps

Main Courses 119

Fry the pork chops to seal the meat. Put them into a dish and cover them with orange juice. Add the ginger and cook in a high oven for half an hour.

Marianne Faithfull
Different Sweet/Sour Pork

Pork fillet
Brown sugar
Garlic, mashed
Lemon, thinly sliced
Salt

Pound garlic and salt. Grill the pork on one side, turn and spread the garlic on the uncooked side, sprinkle liberally with brown sugar and return to the grill. Just before it is cooked, remove from the heat and cover with paper-thin slices of lemon. Grill for a few minutes longer until the lemon becomes soft and delicious.

● We cannot call her winds and waters sighs and tears.
> William Shakespeare
> *Antony and Cleopatra*

Miriam Gross
Fillet of Pork in Cream

Fillet of pork
Cream
Parsley
Thyme

Put the thyme on the fillet and cook it in a medium oven in a tiny bit of water for about 20 minutes. Five minutes before it is done add the parsley and a lot of cream. The pork will be as soft as butter.

Sheila Schülenburg
Vitello Tonnato

Serves 4–6

1 × 7 oz tin tuna fish	*Single cream*
Mayonnaise	*Capers*
Anchovy fillets	*Sliced cold veal (or pork)*

Blend mayonnaise with tuna fish, anchovy fillets and a little single cream and pour over thinly sliced cold veal or pork. Decorate with capers.

This is one of the easiest and quickest recipes from Italy. Buy the sliced veal or pork in the best delicatessen you know. Blending the ingredients for the sauce will only take 2 minutes if you use Hellman's mayonnaise.

Serve with a colourful mixed salad.

A Drinker's Sunday Lunch

Small leg of pork	*1 dessertspoon sugar*
1 red cabbage	*1 teaspoon salt*
1 cooking apple	*1 tablespoon butter*
1 tablespoon vinegar	*New potatoes*
1 clove of garlic	* and another tablespoon butter*

Chop the cabbage and apple and put it in a heavy enamelled casserole. Add the vinegar, garlic, sugar, salt and butter and cover. Rub the pork with oil and salt and wash the potatoes. At 10.30 or 11 – depending on the size of the leg – put the pork in a preheated oven (425F, mark 7) on the top shelf. At 11.30 or 45 – depending on the distance of the pub from the oven – turn the heat down to 400F (mark 6). Put the closely covered cabbage on the middle shelf. Put the potatoes with butter and a little salt in another casserole, cover that closely and put it on the very bottom oven shelf. When you return shortly after 2 p.m. everything should be ready.

Main Courses

- We for a certainty are not the first
  Have sat in taverns while the tempest hurled.

  A. E. Housman (1859–1936)
  A Shropshire Lad

Many people – especially men living alone – always serve the same meal if they have guests. This saves hours of time, thought and anxiety, and if they do it superbly well no one minds in the least. Indeed it is comforting to be able to look forward with pleasure to one's dinner knowing what to expect, and with no fear that your host will surprise you with some outlandish delicacy.

Jean Breech
Leg of Lamb Stuffed with Anchovies

Leg of lamb   Anchovies
Slices of ham

Ask your butcher to remove the bone from the lamb without wrecking the skin. (If he won't do it, avoid this dish, as the deboning is too much trouble.) Roll each slice of ham around a couple of anchovies. Fill up the hollow tunnel inside the lamb with the rolled ham slices. Bake the lamb in the usual way. The anchovies will saturate the meat and make it taste delicious *without* tasting of anchovies.

This dish is very little trouble and has no carving problems.

Mouna Jazzar
Syrian Leg of Lamb

Leg of lamb   Pepper and salt
Garlic   Wine vinegar or lemon juice

Spike leg of lamb with cloves of garlic (as many as possible) and rub it with pepper and salt. Marinate it overnight in vinegar or lemon juice. Turn once. Remove it for 15 minutes, then roast in a moderate oven under tin foil until tender. Serve cold (or hot).

This is a much more exciting cold joint than the usual ham, fowl or beef. It can be prepared the day before. Serve it with brown bread and a salad.

- There's not a thing in the house, the cold mutton having turned with the hot weather.

George and Weedon Grossmith,
Diary of a Nobody (7 June 1888)

Denis Curtis,
Daily Telegraph

Cordero La Chilindron

2 lb boned shoulder of lamb
2 garlic cloves
2 tablespoons olive oil
1 onion
4 oz Parma ham
1 red pimento
12 oz tinned tomatoes

A while back I did a country restaurant tour for the *Telegraph* magazine and one of the pleasures was calling after each meal to interview the owners. I particularly enjoyed talking to Señor Lopez of the Restaurant Elizabeth at Oxford: while we perambulated conversationally he took me through a dozen or more sherries – the driest of which I now serve with a first course of smoked cod's roe instead of a conventional dry white wine. Of course we talked about food and he gave me some peculiarly Spanish recipes including an exotic dish from the Basque area for pheasant in a chocolate sauce. But the concoction which has become a regular part of my repertoire is for a Christmas dish from Navarre: it takes no trouble to prepare and makes an unusual main course for six at luncheon or a weekend supper party. (I have adapted the ingredients to use shoulder of lamb which in quick cooking does not toughen as the originally specified leg, and I use tinned Italian peeled tomatoes which have more flavour than most English fresh varieties.)

Remove excess fat from 2 lb boned shoulder of lamb and cut into $1\frac{1}{2}$ inch cubes. Season. Fry 2 chopped garlic cloves in 2 tablespoons olive oil until golden, add 1 finely chopped onion and then the lamb and 4 oz diced Parma ham and cook for 10 minutes. Add 1 red pimento (skinned and chopped) plus 12 oz tinned tomatoes. Simmer uncovered for 40 minutes. Serve with buttered noodles or rice.

Attic Cutlets

Serves 6

6 lamb cutlets	Tomato purée
2 aubergines	½ cup oil (preferably olive)
2 large onions	Water
6 large potatoes (the yellow Cyprus sort if possible)	Salt

Choose a large, flat, oven-proof dish. Peel and cut the vegetables in half. Arrange them cut side down in between the cutlets. Mix 2 tablespoons of tomato purée with ½ cup of hot water and ½ cup of oil and pour over. Season. Cover and cook until tender. Remove cover to brown meat slightly shortly before the end of the cooking time. Serve with a green bean salad (p. 171).

A small blade bone of pork is also good cooked this way.

Lamb Cutlets in Fresh Lemon Juice

Serves 2

4 lamb cutlets	Salt and pepper
Juice of 1 lemon	Coriander seeds
1 clove of garlic, or marjoram	

Unless you have a large grill, this dish is only little trouble if you are making it for two.

Soak the lamb cutlets in lemon juice for at least 20 minutes. Take out and rub with crushed garlic, or marjoram, and coriander seeds, and season. Cut into edges of meat. Grill 5 minutes each side under a very hot grill. Serve with grilled tomatoes.

You can prepare this for more people if you use a hot oven.

A Quicker, Better Hotpot

Trim most of the fat from some lamb chops – 1 or 2 per person.

Allow 2 potatoes and 1 onion per person and supposing these vegetables to be roughly egg sized, halve them (vegetables cut like this cook faster than if sliced since the heat can more readily circulate around them).

Roughly layer these ingredients in a hotpot casserole, sprinkle with salt and pour over 2 or 3 tablespoons of corn, sunflower or any other polyunsaturated oil. *Add no water.* Cook covered for about an hour (or longer if you are cooking for more than 6) in a hot oven, then remove the cover and cook at the same temperature for a further 15 minutes or until the vegetables are quite soft and crisp on top. Serve with a green vegetable or salad.

Cooked like this the vegetables absorb most of the fat and the polyunsaturated oil makes the dish less greasy than usual – no fat globules floating in watery gravy. It is surprisingly more delicious than conventional hotpot.

Boiled Cook

Under the penalties of Statute 22, Henry VIII, two cooks, viz. John Roose and Margaret Davy, were boiled to death.

● *J'aime la majesté des souffrances humaines.*
Alfred de Vigny (1797–1863)

The Earl of Gowrie
The Earl of Gowrie's Fowl

A pheasant   Garlic Boursin

The art of cooking pheasant is the art of keeping it moist. Some of the best pheasant dishes, therefore, involve elaborate sauces.

The following recipe, which I learnt from a French chef, is an admirable way of cheating, since the pheasant remains moist and is served with the sauce while the cooking and preparation is no more elaborate than it would be with simple roasting.

Stuff the pheasant to capacity with garlic Boursin – this can now be bought at any supermarket. Cover the breast of the bird with a piece of buttered foil and roast on a grid over a roasting pan in a hot oven for 45 minutes. Take the foil off for the last 10 minutes. When the pheasant is cooked, scrape the remaining cheese out of the cavity into the roasting pan and set the pheasant on a carving platter. Pour the cheese and the pheasant juices from the roasting pan into a bowl or a gravy boat and, if it is separated a little, whip with a dash of cream or a yolk of egg – this last step is not usually necessary.

Carve and serve.

- Break a deer, lesche brawn, rear a goose, lift a swan, sauce a capon, frusshe a chicken, spoyle a hen, unbrace a mallard, dismember a heron, display a crane, disfigure a peacock, unjoint a bittern, untach a curlew, allay a pheasant, wing a partridge, wing a quail, mince a plover and thigh a pigeon and other small birds.

Wynkyn de Worde,
Boke of Kervynge (1508)

Sue Lawley
Spicy Chicken

My favourite in the quick, but impressive category is something I call Spicy Chicken (although it is even more successful as Spicy Pheasant):

Serves 4–6

1 chicken
1 pint stock
1 pint double cream
4 tablespoons mushroom ketchup
8 tablespoons Worcestershire sauce
A couple of dashes of tabasco
A couple of teaspoons of made English mustard

Roast a chicken, preferably in a pint of stock with a lump of butter inside the bird – to keep it moist. Let it go cold, skin and joint it. Lay the joints in a shallow dish (about 2 or 3 inches deep), then whizz up a pint of double cream with 4 tablespoons of mushroom ketchup, 8 tablespoons of Worcestershire sauce, a couple of dashes of tabasco and a couple of teaspoons of made English mustard, until thick. Smear it all over the joints and bake it all in a very hot oven for half an hour. The top should turn, will turn, a bubbly golden brown and underneath will be a lovely spicy, creamy sauce of which no one will guess the ingredients (unless you tell them, which you shouldn't). Serve with new potatoes and French beans, to sop up the sauce. Delicious!

● I want every peasant to have a chicken in his pot on Sunday.
    Henri Quatre (1553–1610)

Chicken Cream

Cooked chicken, sliced
Cream
Cucumber, sliced
Parsley sprigs

Put cucumber into cream and heat slowly so as not to separate; then put chicken into sauce so that sauce covers chicken, and heat. Serve garnished with sprigs of parsley.

Gene Baro
Uncle Gene's Chicken Breasts

Serves 6

6 chicken breasts	Nutmeg
Onion	Beaten egg
Butter	Seasoning
Canned artichoke hearts	½ glass white wine
Breadcrumbs	Grand Marnier

Dip 6 boned chicken breasts in beaten egg and roll in fine breadcrumbs to which a generous grating of nutmeg has been added. Sauté slowly in butter – 7 tablespoons for six breasts – in which a finely chopped onion has been yellowed. Season lightly. When the chicken breasts have taken on a golden brown colour, add artichoke hearts (3 or 4 to each breast) and ½ wine glass of dry white wine. When the hearts are heated through, remove them with the chicken breasts to a warm place. Add a tablespoon of Grand Marnier for each chicken breast to the liquor in the pan. Boil up, pour over chicken and serve.

Eat this by itself, with a salad to follow.

William Kennedy
Tandoori Chicken

1 large chicken, jointed   *Tandoori paste (poonam)*

Skin the chicken joints, then cut into the flesh deeply and rub into it ½ or ¾ of a teaspoon of tandoori paste. Heat oven to 450F (mark 8) and cook for 15 to 20 minutes or until the juices are clear. The skin may be rubbed with paste and cooked under the grill. Serve with rice, or poppadoms, and vegetable curry (p. 162).

Jean Breech
Egyptian Chicken

Serves 4–6

3 cloves of garlic   1 cup olive oil
1 lemon   1 chicken in pieces

Grate the lemon peel coarsely and mix with the garlic, the olive oil and the juice of the lemon to make a marinade. Leave the chicken pieces in it all day. When you are ready to cook, put the chicken in a fire-proof dish and cover it with the marinade. Bake for only 20 minutes as the meat will have been broken down by the acid.

Chicken Liver Marsala

Serves 2

½ lb chopped chicken liver (fresh or frozen from Sainsbury's)
Flour for dusting
½ lb chopped onions
1 glass Marsala (or white wine or sherry)
½ cup chicken stock (Knorr)
Butter
Parsley
Salt and pepper
Chopped parsley

Fry the onions in butter until they are golden. Take them out of the pan and fry the chicken livers lightly dusted with flour – quickly in the same fat. Put the onions back into the pan and season. Add one glassful of Marsala – or white wine or sherry – let it bubble and then add half a cupful of chicken stock. Let it simmer on a low heat for another two minutes. Sprinkle with chopped parsley and serve with pasta or rice.

Patricia Thorne
Slapdash Goulash

Serves 2

My husband is a policeman and keeps very odd hours. This is a simple, hot dish which can be prepared in minutes and gives a better impression than a plate of food which has been keeping hot for ages. The rice can be cooked beforehand and heated in a bowl over a pan of boiling water.

2 or 3 breasts of ready-cooked chicken	1 cup rice
Small tin tomato purée	2 tablespoons yoghourt or sour cream
1 clove of garlic, chopped	Parsley
Pinch of mixed herbs	Paprika
Pinch of salt	

Mix the tomato purée with an equal amount of water, the garlic, herbs, and salt. Bring to the boil. Add the chicken breasts, reduce heat and simmer for about 15 minutes. To make it look as though you've really taken trouble, form the rice into rings on the plates and put the chicken mixture in the middle. Add a dollop of yoghourt or sour cream and sprinkle with parsley and a little paprika.

- Salt is the policeman of taste, it keeps the various flavours of a dish in order and restrains the stronger from tyrannizing over the weaker.

    Brillat-Savarin (1755–1826)

Suzy Fleischmann
Chopped Liver

Serves 4

This is a recipe concocted by Jewish *bubahs* for using up all the left-over chicken livers after the compulsory cure-all chicken soup (p. 90).

Main Courses

8 oz chicken livers
1 large onion
1 tablespoon oil or chicken fat (skimmed off the soup)
½ teaspoon mixed herbs
Salt and black pepper
2 large hard-boiled eggs

Fry sliced onion with seasoning until transparent. Add livers and fry gently in covered pan for 8–10 minutes or until cooked. Mince coarsely. Add one minced egg. Garnish with the remaining egg, finely chopped. Serve with matzos or rye crispbread, and salad.

The main recipe varies from house to house – some leave out the first egg and mix in instead matzo meal (or bread-crumbs for *yocks*).

You can also use ox or lamb's liver – or for a vegetable dish, use aubergine instead of meat.

Take a pinch of salt....

One-Dish Chicken

Serves 4–6

3–4 lb chicken	Cloves of garlic
New potatoes	Any other young vegetables
Carrots	Salt and pepper
Spring onions	Butter
Button mushrooms	Fresh herbs

Stuff the chicken with the vegetables and put in the chicken brick. Pack any vegetables that are left over round the chicken, which you have seasoned and smeared with butter. Put extra butter and the herbs in the cavity with the vegetables. Cook in a hot oven for 10 minutes, then lower the heat and cook for a further hour and a half. This dish will keep hot without spoiling for up to a further hour out of the oven as long as you do not raise the lid. Put the brick on a thick wad of newspaper and cover with a heavy folded towel. The meat will shred away from the bones and there will be plenty of well flavoured gravy.

- When I demanded of my friend what viands he preferred,
  He quoth: 'A large cold bottle and a small hot bird!'
  Eugene Field (1850–95)
  The Bottle and the Bird

Victor Haynes
Chicken in Pâté Sauce

Serves 4

1 chicken	1 teaspoon arrowroot
1 tablespoon butter	2 cups chicken stock (Knorr)
Small tin of pâté de foie gras	$\frac{1}{4}$ pint double cream

Buy ready-cooked chicken. Cut into small pieces. Heat a tablespoon of butter in a pan and slowly stir one small tin of *pâté de foie gras* into it. Then gradually add arrowroot to thicken, chicken stock and cream, and heat up chicken pieces in this sauce.

● Your Hen must be perfectly bred as your Cooke ... her head would be smal, her eye very cheerfull and her Crowne armed with a double Cofpel or Crownet.

Markham

Chicken and Salami

Serves 4–6

1 cooked jointed chicken	1 cup wine diluted with
½ lb thinly sliced salami	½ cup water
1 finely chopped spring onion	Grated Gruyère and Parmesan

Put half the salami into a buttered baking dish. Add the roughly sliced spring onion. Put in the chicken pieces. Cover them with the rest of the salami so that they acquire the taste from above and below. Add the wine and water. Sprinkle with grated Parmesan and Gruyère. Bake in a hot oven until the cheese melts, and serve with Cadbury's Smash.

● Fools make feasts and wise men eat them.
Benjamin Franklin (1706–90)

Bertorelli Bros. Restaurant
Pollo alla Cacciatore

Serves 6

3½ lb chicken	1 clove of garlic
1 × 14 oz can peeled tomatoes	3 tablespoons olive oil
¼ pint dry wine	¼ teaspoon basil
6 oz button mushrooms	Salt and pepper
4 oz chopped onion	Chopped parsley
Plain flour	

Divide the chicken into 6 pieces. Heat the oil in a shallow saucepan. Dip the pieces of chicken in the flour and fry until golden all over. Add the crushed garlic, onions, mushrooms, wine. After 10 minutes add tomatoes and basil and the seasoning. Cover and simmer gently until the chicken is tender. Adjust seasoning, add chopped parsley and serve.

American Chicken and Pineapple Salad

Serves 4–6

1 cooked chicken
Mayonnaise (Hellman's, if not home-made)
2 cups diced pineapple (without the juice)
1 clove of garlic, crushed

Combine chicken pieces with mayonnaise, garlic and diced pineapple. Make sure the pineapple pieces are dry, or your mayonnaise will be too runny and too sweet. Drying them on a piece of kitchen paper is quicker than letting the juice drain off in a sieve or colander. Serve with endive or chicory.

- An old gentleman went out to dine. When he got home his sister asked him if he had had a good dinner. He shook his head:
  'If the soup had been as warm as the wine ... If the wine had been as old as the chicken ... If the chicken had been as plump as the cook, I would have had a good dinner.'
  Jewish joke

Duck

Ducks are not too expensive now that they are being intensively reared. They seem grander than mere chicken and are as easy to cook. (Remember you'd need 2 ducks to feed 6 people.)

Duck skin should be very dry before cooking: the best means of achieving this is with a hair drier. Place the prepared duck on a rack and roast in a moderate oven for 1½ hours (some say 40 minutes to the lb), pouring away the fat as it accumulates. Save the fat for roasting potatoes. Check for pink juices by sticking a skewer in the leg. If the juices don't run clear, cook on until they do.

Don't attempt to carve the duck – just cut it into quarters using a strong, non-flexible carving knife.

Accompaniments: stuff the duck with sage and onion and serve it with green peas. Or don't stuff and serve it with orange salad (p. 174). If it's a wild duck serve it with watercress, fried breadcrumbs (p. 77) and game chips – use Smith's crisps heated in the oven.

When baby turnips are in season, boil them until nearly tender in a stock made from the giblets with a teaspoonful of brown sugar added; then roast them round the duck.

Legless Turkey

Come Christmas, cut the legs off a huge turkey (about 22 lb) before cooking. Most people are quite pleased to have only white meat and the bird cooks much more evenly without its legs.

Keep the legs in the fridge for 2 or 3 days, until the memory of roast turkey, turkey salad, turkey sandwiches, turkey soup, etc. has faded somewhat; then marinate them for a few hours in chilli marinade (p. 113) and roast them on a rack in a hot oven for about an hour. Baste occasionally with the marinade during cooking. Serve sliced with hot rice mixed with sultanas plumped up in hot water, sliced almonds, lemon juice and olive oil.

It is always wise to obviate the possibility of too many left-overs since fresh meat is so much more palatable (and safe) than reheated. (You could also deep-freeze the raw legs and serve them for New Year.)

Depending on size, the legs should feed from 4–6.

Blanket of Rabbit

Rabbit is one of the most protein-rich meats – and cheap. There is in this country widespread prejudice against it. Many children (and adults) refuse to eat it because they keep thinking of the Flopsy Bunnies and *Watership Down* (one teenager insists it is not proper food and just like eating budgerigars or guinea pigs) and others think of myxomatosis.

One way of getting round this is not to tell them what they're eating. Freezer stores stock diced boned Chinese rabbit (most rabbit now seems to come from China).

Slightly flour these small anonymous pieces of meat and fry them gently in a little butter with some finely chopped onion – do not brown them. Add the zest and juice of half a lemon and barely enough water to cover. Cook at moderate heat inside the oven for about an hour until the rabbit is tender. Immediately before you serve it, pour in some single cream to make just enough sauce, and season.

Serve with rice or mashed potato and whole green beans. This mixture is also good with button mushrooms in a pie.

The White Tower Restaurant
Courgettes Farcies Avgolemono

Baby marrows (courgettes)   *Lemon juice*
Egg yolks

Stuffing
25% minced lean pork   *Parsley*
75% minced lean beef or lamb   *Mint*
Cooked rice   *Salt and pepper*
Finely chopped onion   *Olive oil*

Empty some courgettes and fry their shells in olive oil gently in a frying pan. Stuff them with the above mixture and place them in a casserole standing up, side by side, with the open end facing upwards. Add stock (or water) to cover the courgettes and cook gently in a slow oven.

Beat some egg yolks and carefully add lemon juice and gravy from the courgettes. The lemon juice should be added drop by drop, otherwise the sauce will curdle. Pour this sauce over the courgettes and serve.

This dish, although delicious, is actually quite a lot of trouble, but can be made the day before. The Greeks and Arabs have a special thing for hollowing out courgettes – it looks like the concave limb of a pair of old-fashioned curling tongs. In place of this an apple corer or a potato peeler can do the job. Stew the scooped out flesh of the courgettes with tomatoes, garlic and oil and serve cold as a first course. (Eds)

- I am acquainted with sad misery
  As the tann'd galley-slave is with his oar.
  John Webster (1580–1625)
  The Duchess of Malfi

May Dinner

Fresh asparagus　　　　*Butter*
New potatoes　　　　　*Chopped parsley*
Westphalian or Parma ham

Steam the asparagus and the unpeeled potatoes. Serve with butter, parsley and the thinnest possible slices of Westphalian or Parma ham.

Follow with the first fresh strawberries and cream.

Tongue Schadenfreude

Canned tongue　　*Chopped onion and browned butter*
Capers

Pour the capers with their juice, and a little chopped onion, which you have softened in brown butter, over sliced tongue. Serve with Dijon mustard and fried courgettes.

It is almost as little trouble to cook an ox tongue as to open a can. Soak it for an hour in cold water whether pickled or not. Choose a round tin or casserole in which it will just fit, curled. Add a bouquet garni and a clove of garlic and cover with water or wine and water. Simmer very slowly in a moderate oven for about 3 hours. Pour off the liquor, skin the tongue and remove the little bones. Press under a plate and weight in the same dish and chill before slicing.

- Cooking is one of those arts which most require to be done by persons of a religious nature.
   Alfred North Whitehead (1861–1947)

Rognons à l'Epicure

Serves 2

1 large can Epicure kidneys	*Butter*
¼ lb roughly chopped mushrooms	*A dash of brandy*
A little chopped onion	*½ glass red wine*

Fry the chopped onion in butter and add mushrooms. Slowly heat up other ingredients in this mixture and serve with a salad.

This is a very good way to cook kidneys. Fresh raw kidneys are time-consuming and unpleasant to prepare. They are bloody and slimy and the knife can slip as one is struggling to remove their disgusting skins and cores.

- Such is life. It is no cleaner than a kitchen; and if you mean to cook your dinner, you must expect to soil your hands; the real art is in getting them clean again, and therein lies the whole morality of our epoch.
   Honoré de Balzac (1799–1850)

Fay Maschler
Kidneys in their Jackets

2–3 kidneys per person

Buy lambs' kidneys that are still in their suet (their fat). A good butcher will have them or might be persuaded to wrench them from his lamb carcasses. Turn on the oven to 350F (mark 4). Place the kidneys in a baking tin and cook in the oven for an hour. The fat will slowly melt and as it is doing so it will be basting the kidneys, which at the end of an hour you remove from any remaining fat, season and serve. As a whole kidney can look a little stark and *physiological* sitting on a plate, it is an idea to serve them tucked inside a baked potato (which you have cooked at the same time), split open and spread with Dijon mustard, or perched astride a mound of puréed parsnip or other root vegetable. A watercress salad completes this practically effortless meal.

Kidneys cooked this way are so meltingly tender and so lacking in any taste associated with their function that even offal haters will be diverted if not converted.

Georgina Howell, Deputy Editor, *Tatler*
Gritty Pasta

Mussels   Cooked pasta
Garlic

After they have been taken out of their shells by the fishmonger,* fry raw mussels for a few minutes in olive oil. Add garlic and throw mussels over pasta.

This sauce has one disadvantage. It sometimes contains a few little bits of grit.

* He'd have to be in love with you to do this. But some fishmongers sell freshly cooked, shelled mussels. (Eds)

Sonia Orwell
Tagliatelli With Truffles

Best tagliatelli *Parmesan*
Cream *Chopped canned truffles*
Butter

Boil the tagliatelli. When they are cooked smother them with cream, Parmesan, a little butter and the truffles. It's the truffles that make this fattening dish so marvellous.

- The Bangala and Bapoto are great man-eaters, but as a rule they do not eat women, considering them much too expensive.

> T. Athol Joyce, M.A. and
> N. W. Thomas, M.A.,
> *Women of all Nations*

Spaghetti Carbonara

Serves 4

1 packet spaghetti 3 tablespoons Parmesan, grated
1 lb ham or bacon Extra Parmesan to serve at table
2 eggs

This is the quickest of the pasta recipes – unless you eat spaghetti with a sauce out of a tin. While the sphaghetti boils in plenty of salted water, cut bacon or ham into thin 1½-inch pieces and fry gently in butter. Drain the spaghetti and put it into a warm dish. Add 2 beaten eggs to the bacon, stir and pour over the spaghetti before the eggs thicken. Stir gently and add Parmesan.

Gully Foges
Pasta with Bacon and Mushrooms

Any kind of pasta (preferably fresh)
Cream
Streaky bacon
Mushrooms
Garlic
Salt and fresh ground black pepper
Parsley

Boil pasta *al dente*. Fry bacon until very crisp. Remove, drain and chop. Fry mushrooms and garlic gently in bacon fat. Then add cream, salt and freshly ground black pepper.

Pour over pasta and sprinkle with lots of chopped parsley on top.

Ann Colcord
Caviar Spaghetti

Serves 4–6

1 lb spaghetti
½ lb melted butter
2 oz pretend caviar (Danish lumpfish roe)

Cook the spaghetti until it is chewy in a great deal of lightly salted water (7 minutes probably). Drain it and add the melted butter and caviar. Add a spoonful of the water from the spaghetti to get all the caviar out of the container. Mix it all well, and serve immediately.

Butterflies and shells of pasta take a bit longer to cook than the spaghetti, but are fun to eat because the caviar clings and makes patterns with the twists of pasta.

Beryl Bainbridge
Stovies

This is a dish my aunt cooked in Liverpool. She called it Stovies, although it is possible, seeing she found it difficult to remember her own name, that it is called something else entirely.

Take 3 lb of potatoes and the contents of a tin of corned beef. (My aunt bought her beef at the butcher's shop and it was dark brown and not the brilliant pink we see now.) Put the potatoes on to boil. It is possible, I suppose, to use several packets of instant mash, but there is really no excuse in this world for not being able to reduce real potatoes to a pulp in 3 minutes flat. All one needs is to turn up the gas, and the ability to detect a smell of burning. Open the tin of corned beef and pull the contents apart. Do not be squeamish. The animal is dead and feels nothing. Drain the potatoes, apply butter and

Do not be squeamish — the animal is dead & feels nothing

season with salt and pepper. Mix in the corned beef, leaving a few colourful shreds poking out of the top. Place under the grill and brown slightly.

To serve in style, arrange a sprig of parsley in the middle and thoughtfully fill a silver gravy boat with Worcestershire sauce.

B.B.'s aunt did get it wrong. The word stovies comes from the French *étuve* and is used by the Scots to describe vegetables (usually potatoes) cooked with a little water or butter in a closed earthenware casserole. (Eds)

- On the Alps it is reported thou didst eat strange flesh.
  William Shakespeare
  Antony and Cleopatra

Theodora FitzGibbon
Torta di Patate

An Italian potato pie which can be whipped up in minutes.

Serves 4–6

- 1 packet instant potato
- 2 oz chopped ham or bacon
- 1 egg yolk and 2 whites
- ½ gill top of the milk
- Salt and pepper
- 3 oz soft cheese, cubed
- 2 tablespoons butter or margarine
- 4 oz dry breadcrumbs

First make up the potato powder, then beat the milk into it, cube the cooked ham or bacon and crush the garlic; then add this to the potato, with the beaten egg yolk. Taste for seasoning, but do not oversalt before adding the cheese, which should be cubed into ¼-inch size, then folded in. Finally stiffly beat the egg whites and gently mix them in.

Heat the butter to foaming; then quickly fry the breadcrumbs. Grease a cake tin with removable base, and coat it with most of the breadcrumbs, leaving enough to top. Pour the potato mixture into the tin. Then cover with the remaining crumbs, and put into the centre of a hot oven (400F, mark 6) for about 20 minutes. When cooked, turn out on to a warmed plate and serve cut into wedges like a cake, which is what it will look like. The ham can be omitted for vegetarians, and it is a delicious dish.

William Kennedy
Beef and Bacon Loaf

Serves 6

1 lb beef ⎱ minced
1 lb bacon ⎰
6 oz breadcrumbs
½ grated nutmeg
½ teaspoon mace and pepper to taste
2 beaten eggs
A hard-boiled egg may be enclosed if desired

Mix all ingredients together, binding with the beaten egg. Cook in a low oven in a closely covered oval or rectangular dish in a baking pan of water for 2½ hours. Press when cooked and leave to cool.

This is the quickest and easiest of meat loaves – the fatty bacon flavours and moistens the beef.

Ann Dunn
Cold Omelette

Liver
Fresh cream
Seasoning
Eggs
Tomato purée
Olives

Fry a couple of slices of liver. Put in mixer with fresh cream, reduce to light purée, add salt and pepper. Make omelette and add this filling. Fold over and cover with tomato purée and chopped olives. Serve cold. A good summer lunch dish.

Dido Merwyn
Dido's Omelette

2 good handfuls of sorrel
3 or 4 Petit Suisse cream cheeses
6 eggs
2 heaped teaspoons of butter
1 clove of garlic
Grated nutmeg
Tabasco
Salt

To make filling: wash and then warm in butter for a few minutes the chopped sorrel, from which the stalks have been removed. Drain well and press free of moisture. Add a clove of garlic and blend with 3 or 4 Petit Suisse cheeses. Season with salt to taste and plenty of grated nutmeg. Make a six-egg omelette well seasoned with tabasco. When ready, spread the filling over half of the omelette and fold over the other half.

To make a more substantial dish, add chopped lean ham to the omelette before spreading the filling.

Another good variant can be made by adding chopped walnuts instead of ham, in which case the nutmeg should be omitted from the filling.

Theodora FitzGibbon
Soufflé

Serves 2

If you use a packet sauce mix with half the milk stated then it makes an excellent base for a soufflé: cheese or mushroom sauce is good for this. Cool for a minute or two when it's made up. Then stir in two egg yolks and finally the stiffly beaten egg whites. Put into a lightly greased dish and bake at 375F (mark 5) for approximately 25 minutes, then serve at once.

Natasha Spender
Cheese and Onion Soufflé

Serves 4

1½ lb chopped onions
6 oz grated cheese
6 eggs
Salt
Pinch of dry mustard
2 oz butter
Black pepper

I always have Cheddar cheese and onions in my larder. In the panic of unexpected guests I serve this soufflé, which can be made with little trouble. Simmer the chopped onions in the butter in a heavy closed casserole until they are transparent. Add the beaten yolks of six eggs, the stiffly whipped whites, and the cheese (grated). Mix thoroughly and put in a soufflé dish with a little salt and lots of black pepper. When your last guest arrives cook the soufflé at 375F (mark 5) until risen and lightly browned.

We were astonished to read this and realise it required no béchamel or panada base – it sounded at first like a vertical omelette – so we made it, and it works like a dream and is delicious. (Eds)

● They say miracles are past.
William Shakespeare
All's Well That Ends Well

Ukrainian Eggs

Serves 4

8 eggs
1 onion
½ cup oil
1 teaspoon paprika
1 cup sour cream

Fry sliced onion in oil, add paprika and sour cream. Stir well and pour into oven-proof dish. Break eggs into this sauce and bake in oven until set.

Minn Hogg,
Fashion Editor, *Sheba* magazine

Smashed Eggs

Smash Eggs   Parmesan cheese

Place a layer of Smash in a flat dish and make dents in it. Fill the dents with raw eggs. Cover with a sloppy layer of Smash plus a packet of Parmesan cheese. Cook in the oven or under the grill until the eggs set.

Minn Hogg

Travelling Bacon Recipe

Turn your steam-iron up to 'linen'. Place slices of streaky bacon (preferably Dane-Pack) on hand-held upturned iron. This makes the bacon very crisp and unfattening as the fat drips down the apertures in the iron.

This ist ein joke. (Eds)

Gladys Mary Coles

Poet's Pie

My husband arrived home unexpectedly (after previously telling me he was spending the night in Manchester) and he arrived complete with a very important guest (minus pyjamas but plus briefcase) – what to give them to eat when I had catered only for the children's beans on toast and supermarket yoghourt? In the fridge I had some frozen green beans, ½ dozen eggs, 2 slices of ham, and some frozen short pastry. Pastry hastily unfrozen and bludgeoned into shape by rolling pin, eggs hastily scrambled (never to be unscrambled, how can one unscramble an egg?).* Right: eggs scrambled, laid in flan dish with pastry and topped by ham strips; pastry has already been cooked quickly on top of the oven without being made into tasteless toast, frozen green beans have been rapidly prepared, strained off, lying limp and recalcitrant in my orange colander – now to reach their artistic heights, their *raison d'être*, laid in criss-cross pattern across the exotic flan. Can be topped (if you have it) by grated cheese and slices of tomato for an aesthetic touch of colour!

- *Ite domum saturae, venit Hesperus, ite capellae.*
  (Get ye home, my full-fed goats, get ye home – the Evening Star draws on!)

Virgil (70–19 B.C.)
Eclogue, x

---

* Professor Richard Gregory, Director of the Institute of Brain and Perception, suggests that a short answer to this entropic dilemma would be to feed this dish to a hen. (Eds)

Sauces

> In Nature's infinite book of secrecy
> A little I can read.
>
> William Shakespeare
> *Antony and Cleopatra*

Francis Bacon
Thick, Fat, Genuine Mayonnaise

1 egg   ½ pint olive oil

Break the yolk of an egg on to a flat plate. Throw away the white. Use about 6 oz to ½ pint of good olive oil to the yolk of egg. Stir vigorously. As soon as the yolk and oil begin to emulsify, the oil can be added more rapidly. This makes the best mayonnaise. If possible don't add vinegar, lemon or mustard, just very little salt.

The easiest way to separate an egg is to break it into your hand, let the white trickle through your fingers, and pull away the membranous strings. If you use a large shallow dish it doesn't matter so much if you pour in more oil than you intended since you simply tip the dish so that the oil slides away from the emulsion and you can scoop up as little as you like and carry on mixing (a large fork is best).

Although a food processor and some very fast blenders make perfect mayonnaise with a whole egg, for the hand-made sort even a touch of white means disaster.

The Spanish have a special oil pourer for mayonnaise but it seems you have to go to Spain to get it. (Eds)

● There is superstition in avoiding superstition.
Francis Bacon (1561–1626)
Essay, of Superstition

Nicholas Haslam
Fake Mayonnaise for Masking Cold Chicken

Equal parts Hellman's mayonnaise and sour cream. Add a chicken stock cube melted in as little hot water as possible.

Nicholas Haslam
Fake Hollandaise

Add 1 egg yolk per cup of Hellman's mayonnaise. Add good vinegar to taste.

Nicholas Haslam
Fake Maltaise

As above but add juice of 1 orange.

● Mayonn-aise have seen the glory of the coming of the Lord.
Old joke

Quick Hollandaise

Put two egg yolks in the blender and whizz them once. Melt ½ lb of butter and pour it on to the yolks, blending at full speed. Add salt, pepper and lemon juice to taste. Serve at once.

Jennifer Ross
Salsa Verde

Chop up capers, anchovies, garlic and parsley. Mix these ingredients into a thick French dressing. This is an excellent sauce to liven up any left-over meats.

Onion Sauce

Buy a packet of frozen baby onions in cream sauce. Make up according to directions then blend. Add a pinch of powdered cloves.

Helen Jones
Mint Jelly

Take four little squares of a lime or lemon jelly and melt them in one tablespoon of hot water. Add to this one heaped tablespoon of finely chopped mint (or 4 teaspoons of concentrated mint sauce). Add one or two teaspoons of vinegar and let set.

A Sauce For Fish

Mix fresh lime or lemon juice into plain yoghourt and season with salt and pepper.

Another

Thicken some single cream with a little lemon juice or wine vinegar. Add a teaspoon of made English mustard and season with salt and pepper. Be careful not to curdle the mixture.

Sauce for Ducks

Half a jar of morello cherry jam with the juice of ½ a lemon and 2 wine glasses of red wine. Boil until reduced slightly.

Mock Horseradish

Finely grate 2 medium-sized carrots, sprinkle them with 2 teaspoons of English mustard, 1 scant teaspoon of salt, and 2 or 3 teaspoons of caster sugar. Moisten with wine vinegar and mix well. Add 1 or 2 dessertspoons of single cream. Good with steak or hamburger.

Mrs Richard Ryan
Barbecue Sauce

½ cup soy sauce diluted with ¼ cup water
3 cloves of garlic
3 chopped spring onions, or 1 chopped leek
1 teaspoon fresh ginger, chopped
1½ teaspoons sugar

Use as a marinade for fish or meat.

It's vintage '79

Vanna Cooper
Vanna's Italian Spaghetti Sauce

½ lb meat for mincing
Small tin tomatoes
1 onion
1 clove of garlic
Good pinch thyme or mixed herbs

Mince ½ lb meat together with one onion and place without any oil in a saucepan. Steam on very low heat for ½ hour. Then add a small tin of tomatoes, a crushed clove of garlic and some basil. Season and simmer for another ¼ hour. The result is delicious, the taste is authentic, but without ALL THAT OIL.

Fay Maschler
Anchovy Sauce for Baked Fish or Boiled Vegetables

This extraordinarily easy sauce will embellish a reasonably priced fish like grey mullet or red bream baked in the oven, and is also excellent served with vegetables for a first course.

1 tin anchovy fillets
2 oz butter
1 medium-sized carton double cream
Freshly ground black pepper

Soak the anchovy fillets briefly in a saucer of warm water. Drain off. Melt the butter in a shallow pan. Add the anchovy fillets and stir around until they break up. Tinned anchovies when subjected to heat completely fall apart. Add the cream and boil up while stirring until the mixture amalgamates. Season with pepper. The anchovies will have taken care of the saltiness. This sauce has an elusive, impressive flavour.

Butters or Hard Sauces

Use unsalted butter and season to taste.

Garlic Butter

Mince peeled cloves of garlic (2 or 3 to 4 oz butter) in a blender or food processor, then add the butter cut into pieces, salt, black pepper and a squeeze of lemon juice. Firm in the fridge to serve with steaks, grilled chicken, boiled potatoes, etc.

Anchovy Butter

Rinse six or seven anchovies and blend them. Add 4 oz butter cut into pieces. Add lemon juice to taste, but no salt.

Prawn Butter

Take $\frac{1}{4}$ pint of peeled prawns and proceed as for Anchovy Butter. If the butter looks a little pale, add a teaspoon of tomato purée. Season to taste.

Green Butter

Mince a handful of parsley (washed and well dried) with chives (or a bit of onion) and any other fresh herbs. Add lemon juice and salt. You can also use 1 or 2 fresh spinach leaves. Add 4 oz butter, cut into pieces, and blend. Use with pasta, potatoes, fish, etc. Substitute cottage or cream cheese for the butter to serve with baked potatoes.

Brandy Butter

4 oz unsalted butter
2 oz icing sugar
2 oz caster sugar
Grated rind of $\frac{1}{2}$ orange
2 tablespoons brandy

Mix all together in a blender. It has been discovered that this will keep (tightly wrapped and sealed, in the fridge) from Christmas to Christmas.

Vegetables and Salads

> Wherefore do ye spend money for that which is
> not bread?
>
> *Isaiah*, lv.1

Vegetable Casserole

This is a most delicious winter dish in itself and needs no accompaniment. Take any root vegetables that you like (except beetroot which would discolour the others), peel and cut them into smallish chunks (not slices). Add quartered onions and garlic cloves, seasoning and a little butter. Put into a heavy earthenware casserole and cover closely (add no water). Cook very slowly for several hours. Make a thick cheese sauce and add to it the liquid which the vegetables will have made. Pour this over the vegetables, sprinkle the top with butter, and sizzle under the grill. Serve a cold first course of fish, or meat pâté.

Ratatouille

Serves 6

½ lb green or red peppers	½ lb aubergines
½ lb onions	Cloves of garlic
½ lb tomatoes	Sea salt
½ lb courgettes	1 cup olive oil

Peel and chop onion. Slice, but do not peel tomatoes, courgettes and aubergines. Add garlic, and season. Cover the vegetables closely, adding no water, and stew them slowly in the oil until they are melted.

This is best served lukewarm. On no account chill: it would destroy the flavour.

Many Mediterranean and Middle Eastern dishes are best served lukewarm. The English passion for piping hot food results partly from the lack of centrally heated dining rooms in winter, and partly from the fact that the English have traditionally cooked with meat fat, which congeals horribly when cold.

Potatoes in their Jerseys

Take tiny new Jersey potatoes and wash them well but do not scrape. Steam or boil them. Rub a cut clove of garlic round individual, ovenproof bowls or ramekins. Put a few potatoes in each and cover with thick cream. Sprinkle over them grated cheese, black pepper, breadcrumbs and bits of butter. Heat through in the oven or under the grill and serve as a separate course or with meat. They give a very fancy impression and take almost no time to cook.

Waistcoat Potatoes

You don't have to choose enormous potatoes to bake in their skins – they take at least an hour to cook. You can bake little ones or big ones cut in half – the cut side forms a crusty skin. You can't stuff these small potatoes, but you can serve them piping hot with Boursin or cream cheese and chopped chives and parsley melting over them.

(To cook large potatoes more quickly, stick a skewer or metal knitting needle through each lengthways.)

Vegetable Curry

Serves 4

1 tin tomatoes
Chopped or dried onion
Handful frozen mixed vegetables
1 tablespoon oil for frying
Cold cooked potato if possible
Curry powder
Salt

Fry fresh, or soak dried onion. Add tomatoes and boil. Stir in curry powder mixed to a paste with a little water. Add vegetables and simmer until cooked and the liquid is slightly reduced. Serve over hot shelled hard-boiled eggs, or with tandoori chicken (p. 128).

Fay Maschler
Spiced Parsnips

Serves 4

1 lb parsnips
1 oz butter
1 tablespoon vegetable oil
1 teaspoon turmeric
1 level teaspoon cumin seeds
1 level teaspoon coriander seeds
½ teaspoon fenugreek
The seeds of 5 cardamom pods
1 scant teaspoon black mustard seeds
1 dried red chilli, if you wish hotness
Fresh coriander, parsley or watercress leaves
Salt, pepper, lemon juice for seasoning

Since I keep a supply of most Indian spices (easy enough to assemble) the ingredients are, to some extent, a reflection of my shelves. You can vary the spices without the dish coming to harm, but cardamom and turmeric should not, I feel, be omitted. But if fenugreek is not at your local shop it doesn't really matter.

Peel the parsnips and cut as if you were making chips – in half horizontally, then quartered vertically. Heat the mixture of butter and oil in a shallow pan or frying pan to which you can fit a lid. Add the cumin, coriander, fenugreek, cardamom, mustard seeds and chilli (optional), and fry until the seeds begin to pop, which they will do rapidly. Add the turmeric and stir some more until you have a loose paste. Add the parsnips and turn in the spicy mixture until they are covered and coloured. Add a couple of tablespoons of warm water and cook, covered, watching and adding more water in dribs and drabs until the parsnip pieces are tender (about 20 minutes). Chop finely some fresh coriander leaves or parsley or watercress leaves and add, shaking the pan about. Season with salt and pepper and lemon juice and if there is water left in the pan, evaporate through brisk cooking. Serve with plain yoghourt and fried poppadoms as a course on its own, or it makes an enlivening vegetable with any meat, not necessarily curried, though it went very well, I found, with curried chicken livers.

Curried Mushroom and Nuts

Rice (brown)
Nuts (any type you prefer)
Mushrooms
Curry powder
Garlic
Onions
Oil

Fry garlic, onions and curry powder (with a little liquid) to make a sauce. Add nuts (sliced), then add sliced mushrooms and fry very gently so as not to overcook. Serve on a bed of rice with a green salad.

Zita Mulhern
Quicker Than Quick Veg

Serves 4

1 onion
1 pepper, green or red
A few sticks of celery
1 clove of garlic, crushed
1 can tomatoes
Butter
Salt and black pepper

Peel and slice onion, slice pepper and celery and crush garlic. Fry onion and garlic gently in butter and add pepper and celery. Toss together for a minute. Add tomatoes and season. Cook until heated through, but it is important that vegetables stay crisp.

Stir-Fried Cabbage

Serves 4

Small Chinese, savoy, white or any crisp cabbage
1 small onion, or garlic
1 tablespoon oil
Bacon if desired

Wash and finely slice the cabbage. Chop the onion. Heat the oil, and add the onion. Stir for a moment, then add the cabbage and stir and turn constantly until the cabbage is heated through – it should stay crisp. Use a *wok* or heavy iron frying pan.

Sprouts and broccoli can also be cooked this way – finely sliced; also well washed young nettles.

Hot Potato Salad

Serves 4

$\frac{1}{2}$ lb onion
3 sticks celery
2 lb cooked potatoes
6 oz diced cooked ham
Oil
A little French dressing

Stir-fry the chopped onion and celery in the oil for a minute or two, then add the diced potato and ham. Heat through. The celery should stay slightly crisp. Pour over an oily French dressing.

Charlotte Bielenberg
Red Cabbage and Frankfurters

Serves 6

1 red cabbage
2 apples
2 onions
2 cloves of garlic
2 tablespoons vinegar
$1\frac{1}{2}$ cups wine or water
Salt and sugar
Frankfurters

Fry the onions in a mixture of butter and oil. When they are soft, pour in the shredded red cabbage and stir. Add peeled and chopped apples and all other ingredients. Boil in a pressure cooker for 15 minutes, or let it simmer in a very low oven, with a tight lid on it, for 2 hours.

The cabbage will be much better if you heat it up the next day. Serve with frankfurters.

George Mott
Baked Fennel

Calculate one head per person as a first course, less as a side dish. Wash thoroughly and cut off the stalks. Cut a deep gash in the top and remove a small wedge. Fill with 4 or 5 green peppercorns (*poivre vert*), a teaspoon of *aceto balsamico* (or an aromatic mild vinegar), a pinch of oregano, pepper and salt. Put in a casserole dish and cover each head of fennel with a generous tablespoon of good olive oil. Cover and cook for about 40 minutes or until tender. Before serving ladle the juice over the fennel; also good cold.

Baked Onions

Rinse large onions and bake them in the oven in their skins. When they are meltingly soft, serve as a separate course with cold butter, salt and freshly milled white pepper.

Spinach and Bacon Salad with Hot Honey

Serves 4

$1\frac{1}{2}$ *lb spinach (raw)*   *4 teaspoons hot honey*
1 lb streaky bacon   *Vinaigrette*

Wash and clean spinach, and chop, but not too finely. Cook bacon until very crispy, cool, and chop finely. Place spinach in salad dishes. Sprinkle with bacon. Pour hot honey over salad. Serve with vinaigrette dressing.

Ann Dunn
Variation on Piperade

Courgettes   *Parsley*
Olive oil   *Garlic*
Eggs   *Seasoning*

Gently fry chopped young courgettes in olive oil with chopped parsley and garlic. Break in 2 eggs per person and stir rapidly until completely amalgamated with the vegetable. Add salt and plenty of pepper and serve directly out of frying pan.

Brown Lentil Stew *Hausfrauenart*

Serves about 10

1 lb brown lentils (soaked overnight, and rinsed before cooking)	1 cube Knorr chicken stock
2 onions, roughly chopped	$\frac{1}{2}$ lb streaky smoked rashers of bacon
2 carrots, peeled and sliced	A lot of water
2 potatoes	2 tablespoons tomato concentrate
2 cloves of garlic	
1 bay leaf	

The list of ingredients looks lengthy and off-putting, but it only takes 10 minutes to get them all together. Just throw them all in a cook-pot, stir and cover. This recipe can be made in the large Kenwood Cook-Pot, which holds $8\frac{3}{4}$ pints. You can let the vegetables simmer in this slow-cooking device for half a day or a whole day.

Serve with frankfurters from your best delicatessen, or the German Food Centre, if you live in London.

Grandma's Dish

Small new potatoes *Peas or beans*
Onions *Bacon, thinly sliced*
Carrots

Put the vegetables in a steamer or pressure cooker and cover with the (rindless) slices of bacon. Do not peel the well washed potatoes and carrots, and (depending on the salinity of the bacon) do not add salt. The bacon will be cooked when the vegetables are tender.

Mouna Jazzar
Hummus

½ lb chick peas *Salt*
2–4 cloves of garlic *Parsley*
4 tablespoons tahini *Cumin seed*
Juice of 2 lemons *Paprika*

Soak the chick peas overnight. Simmer them in a pressure cooker for an hour. Blend them (preferably in a Magimix) with the garlic, the tahini, lemon juice and salt, until perfectly smooth. Pour the hummus into a shallow dish and decorate it with parsley, cumin seed and paprika in rows.

You can buy tinned hummus but soaking and simmering are not actually any trouble.

Mouna Jazzar
Baba Ghanouch (Dad's Treat)

Bake a large aubergine and scoop out the flesh. Proceed exactly as for hummus, adding a spoonful of plain yoghourt. Remember to score the aubergine twice with a sharp knife, or it will explode in the oven. Bang.

Mouna Jazzar
Pepper Dip

1 can red peppers
¼ lb shelled walnuts
Small onion (or ½ a larger one)
Juice of 1 lemon
A pinch of cumin

Salt
1 slice dry toast
Olive oil ⎫ *optional*
Pine nuts ⎭

Rinse the peppers, and blend all the ingredients (Mouna Jazzar uses a mincer for this dish rather than the Magimix – it should not be too fine; there should be pieces of walnut evident).

Sometimes the Syrians use concentrated pomegranate juice instead of lemon, but this is difficult to obtain here. You can add a little olive oil and decorate with pine nuts.

Serve with hot pitta bread as a first course, or use for canapés, or as a dip.

All these dips make a very easy first course since they require no cutlery – no plates either if guests don't mind dipping their pitta into the communal dish. (Eds)

Bernard Shaw's Vegetarian Salads

Date and Nut
Leaves of lettuce, blobs of cream cheese decorated with salted nuts, chopped dates and raisins served with a dressing made of olive oil, fresh lemon juice, sugar (soft brown), pepper and sea salt.

Cauliflower and Tomato
A well cooked cauliflower served cold on tender cabbage leaves decorated with a chopped green pepper and sliced peeled tomatoes and nuggets of garlic, with a dressing made of cider vinegar, olive oil, salt and red pepper.

Mixed Salad
Shredded lettuce, hard-boiled eggs, cold sliced potatoes, peeled tomatoes, parsley, peeled and sliced apples, sultanas, shredded Cheddar, sliced radishes, cooked but cold carrots, chopped onions – the whole mixed with a home-made mayonnaise, riddled with pepper from a mill.

These were Shaw's favourite salads. The cider in the vinegar was the only alcohol he allowed himself.

Nasturtium Salad
Wash a lettuce and 6 large unblemished nasturtium leaves. Tear them into bits, dress with vinaigrette and add some nasturtium seeds. Decorate with nasturtium flowers.

Liz Calder
Burgul Salad

1 lb burgul *or cracked wheat*
Some chopped onion
Lemon juice

Chopped parsley and mint
Salt and pepper

Soak *burgul* in water for ½ an hour. It will swell considerably. Squeeze water out with your hands and spread on a tea towel to dry out for a further ½ hour.

Add some finely chopped onion and lashings of lemon juice, chopped parsley and mint, salt and pepper. A terrific party basic.

Tomato Salad

1 lb tomatoes *Vinaigrette*
1 teaspoon chopped fresh tarragon

Slice the unpeeled tomatoes very thinly, put in a shallow dish and cover with tarragon and a little vinaigrette. Or peel and quarter the tomatoes and place in a deep bowl with a slightly warmed, very oily and garlicky dressing.

These two salads are entirely different in character. The second can be served as a separate course with French or Greek bread.

Green Bean Salad

Green beans *1 can tomatoes*
1 onion *Olive oil*

Soften chopped onion in olive oil. Add a packet of frozen whole French beans and turn them well. Add a small can of tomatoes and cook until the beans are tender.

Serve cold as a first course with bread, or as a salad with cold meat, or as a light supper with tuna fish softened with cream, lemon juice, salt and black pepper.

Peasants' Salad

Finely chopped green pepper
Finely shredded lettuce
3 hard, chopped tomatoes
Finely chopped onions
Chopped cucumber
Chopped radishes
* and any salad*
* stuff you have*

Mix it all up with pounded garlic, lemon juice, salt, pepper, chopped mint, parsley and powdered cumin.
   This has to be eaten with a spoon.

Mushrooms à la Grecque

Button mushrooms (can be tinned)
Tomato purée
Vinaigrette
A dash of tabasco

Rinse some fine button mushrooms under the cold tap. Steam or boil for one minute, and then plunge them into cold water. Dress them with a vinaigrette, to which you have added one tablespoon of tomato purée and a dash of tabasco.

Rachel and Jonathan Miller
Saturday Salad

The basic ingredients of this salad are celery, apple,* cheese, cashew nuts and currants. The first three are cut into cubes less than ½ inch across. The dressing consists of 3 tablespoons olive oil to 1 tablespoon wine vinegar, ⅓ teaspoon mustard powder, 1 teaspoon sugar, salt and pepper, garlic and fennel seeds. However, the thing about Saturday is that people tend to turn up unexpectedly for lunch, so the salad has to get bigger. You

---

* You can use up the apples that no one will eat because they're bruised. Leave the peel on, as this adds colour to the salad.

can do this by doubling the quantities or by adding more things – depending on what there is – raw red or white cabbage, carrots, fennel, celeriac, chicory, cottage cheese, cold rice, and anything else you can think of.

- It's my old girl that advises. She has the head. But I never own to it before her. Discipline must be maintained.
  Charles Dickens (1812–70)
  Bleak House

Coleslaw

White cabbage   1 mild onion
1–2 carrots   Mayonnaise
1–2 apples

Peel the onion and wash the other things. Chop or slice finely and mix with mayonnaise. You can use red cabbage – very dramatic.

Mary Lefcowitz
Waldorf Salad

Equal quantities of chopped   Mayonnaise to bind
* celery and apple   Seedless grapes*
Chopped walnuts

Mix together celery, apple and mayonnaise. Garnish with walnuts and grapes.

- Let the salad maker be a spendthrift for oil, a miser for vinegar, a statesman for salt, and a madman for mixing.
  Spanish proverb

Carrot and Garlic Salad

Coarsely grated carrots
Fresh lemon juice
Olive oil

2 cloves of garlic, crushed
Sugar, salt and pepper

Mix up all ingredients at least 1 hour before eating the salad.

Cucumber Salad

1 cucumber
1 clove of garlic
Lots of mint, freshly chopped
Parsley

1 carton plain yoghourt
Salt
Black pepper

Slice the cucumber. Chop the garlic, mint, and parsley. Season and add yoghourt. Chill.

Another

Finely slice a cucumber and sprinkle with sugar, salt, pepper and lemon juice to taste. Sprinkle with mint.

Orange and Onion Salad

Finely slice peeled oranges and Spanish onions. Sprinkle with sea salt, olive oil and a little lemon juice. Dot with black olives.
   Divine with duck.

Salade Niçoise

Take a crisp lettuce, such as a Webb's Wonder. Wash and dry thoroughly. Arrange in a large bowl with quartered hard tomatoes, spring onions, olives, tuna fish, quartered hard-boiled eggs and whole cooked green beans. Sprinkle with a vinaigrette dressing just before serving – but do not attempt to toss the salad.

You may add other vegetables to this classic salad – chopped green peppers, cucumber, small whole Jersey potatoes, gherkins, etc.

This is usually thought of as a first course, which is a bit silly when you consider how much you can get into it.

Russian Salad

Frozen mixed vegetables *Chopped onion or celery*
Mayonnaise *(optional)*

Cook the vegetables according to the packet directions. If you are making a large quantity for a party, cook them in several batches or they will not boil quickly enough and will go soggy. As with a potato salad, add the mayonnaise while the vegetables are still warm.

Bean Salad

Take any dried beans – white, black, brown or red. Soy beans are good as they always retain a certain bite. Cover well with boiling water and soak overnight. Rinse, and simmer until tender. Do not add salt until the end of the cooking, otherwise the beans will be tough. Dress with vinaigrette and add chopped onion, parsley, other herbs, or olives. Add extra oil if they seem dry.

Puddings

Kissing don't last: cookery do!
> George Meredith (1828–1909)
> *The Ordeal of Richard Feverel*

> But men must know, that in this theatre of man's life it is reserved only for God and angels to be lookers on.
>
> Francis Bacon (1561–1626)
> *Advancement of Learning*

Mrs Heather Brigstocke, M.A., High Mistress of St Paul's Girls' School
Kiwi Fruit Ice

Serves 6

6 Kiwi fruit (or Chinese gooseberries, as they were once known)
Juice of 1 lemon
½ pint of water
3 oz sugar
5 oz single cream

A Magimix is essential for this. Peel and cut up the Kiwi fruit, and boil the sugar in the water to make a syrup. Put the fruit and lemon juice in the blender, and mix well. Blend in the cream and cool syrup and turn into a mould and freeze. When it is half frozen, beat it again in the mould and finish freezing. Serve with thin rich biscuits such as *langues de chat*.

M. Jacques Viney, F.C.F.A., A.C.F., Chef at the Ritz
La Pêche de Bacchus or Pêches au Champagne

Serves 4

6 ripe peaches (not too ripe)
¼ bottle champagne (or Pomagne)
3 oz caster sugar
Juice of 1 lemon and 1 orange plus the zest of both
Orange sorbet

Dip the peaches in a pan of boiling water for a few seconds so that you can peel them very easily, then cut them in halves following the depression around the fruit. Take stones out and slice with a sharp stainless steel knife or silver knife (the juice of the peaches oxidates other knives and makes black stains on the slices), making 4 equal slices in each half. Put the peaches in a glass serving bowl. Sprinkle with sugar, lemon and orange juice, make a very fine julienne of the rind of both fruits (do not use too much), then mix well but gently so as not to bruise the peach slices, for the rind to be equally distributed amongst the peaches. Pour the $\frac{1}{4}$ bottle of champagne or Pomagne over the sliced peaches.

Chill for about 4 hours before serving. It will make a delightful end to a sumptuous meal.

Also you may serve an orange sorbet.

In some spheres of the upper crust they add a measure of curaçao; it makes this dessert a perfection.

Peaches and Raspberries

Take perfectly ripe peaches, scald them and remove the skins. Halve them and remove the stones. Into the hollow pour a purée of fresh or frozen raspberries blended with caster sugar and sieved.

Raspberry Ice and Fire

Serves 4

1 lb frozen raspberries	1 pint water
Powdered gelatine (quantity given on packet)	4–5 tablespoons sugar

Take rather more than the right amount of gelatine and melt it in 1 pint of hot water. Add the sugar and stir. Pour in frozen raspberries. The fruit will instantly melt while the gelatine syrup will instantly set.

Cara Denman
Another

Serves 4

*1 packet frozen blackcurrants or
   frozen raspberries*
Sugar

Put the frozen fruit in the Magimix or blender. Add sugar to taste. Mash it up until it becomes a paste. This makes a refreshing and tart dessert rather like a sorbet. It should be served in a glass with cream. The fruit is better mashed before dinner, so it can thaw a little, otherwise it is too cold and might give guests indigestion.

- This was a good dinner enough, to be sure; but it was not a dinner to *ask* a man to.
  Dr Johnson (1709–84)
  Boswell's *Life*

Melon Framboise

Serves 6

1 melon   *Kirsch or brandy*
1 lb raspberries *Caster sugar*

Dice scooped-out melon meat and combine with fresh raspberries, add kirsch or brandy, and chill. Serve sugar separately, as most people are trying to slim. You can serve this fruit salad in the scooped out melon, but it looks a bit gimmicky and is inclined to topple over.

Once-a-Year Fruit Salad

Seedless grapes when in season
Thinly sliced Granny Smith
 apples (with skin on them)
Sliced bananas
1 tablespoon lemon juice
Preserved ginger in syrup

Pour ginger syrup and lemon juice over the fruit and sprinkle with little bits of ginger.

Make this fruit salad at the last minute, otherwise the bananas will go brown. The contrasts of texture and flavour make this most unusual and refreshing. If possible sprinkle some tiny chips of ice over just before serving.

David Cheshire
Grape Salad

Seedless grapes   Brown sugar

Slice the grapes. Leave them to marinate in brown sugar. They will create their own sweet juice, which is very good. Serve them with sour cream as a contrast.

Lady Stuart
Stewed Rhubarb

Rhubarb   Honey
Brown sugar

Place all the ingredients in a saucepan and cook without any water. They will create their own delicious juice. Simmer on a very low flame for about 15 minutes.

I once made this pudding for some people, and when they came again a few weeks later they said, 'Darling, do let's go out.'

Rum Banana

Slice peeled bananas lengthways. Put them in an oven-proof dish. Cover thickly with brown sugar. Sprinkle with lemon juice and rum. Sizzle quickly under the grill or cook for $\frac{1}{4}$ of an hour in a moderate oven. Serve with thick chilled cream.

This dish can also be made by frying the bananas gently in butter on top of the cooker.

Banana Cream

Serves 4

4 ripe bananas *1 cup chopped walnuts*
2 cups cream *Crushed ice*
1$\frac{1}{2}$ tablespoons sugar

Put all ingredients and some crushed ice into the blender and blend well.

It should be eaten immediately after you have made it.

Lady Antonia Fraser
Banana Dessert
(Made at the last minute)

Bananas *Ice cubes*
Yoghourt *White rum (optional)*
Sugar

My least troublesome recipe is a banana dessert. Put all the ingredients in the blender with lots of ice cubes. Add white rum if you want this dessert to taste 'special'. When the mixture turns to a cream foam, pour it into wine goblets. Wine goblets are important because they help to prevent the banana cream from sagging and also look impressive. Decorate every goblet with a strip of banana if the mixture is not sagging too badly to hold it.

- And solid pudding against empty praise.

    Alexander Pope (1688–1744)
    The Dunciad

Day and Richard Wollheim
Yule Log

1 large tin Purée de marrons nature Clement Faugier
4 oz bitter chocolate
2 tablespoons milk
Vanilla or coffee essence – or both
5 oz sugar

5 oz butter
A few drops of drink, if available
Candied fruit or whipped cream
Chocolate shavings

Melt the chocolate in the milk with the vanilla and/or coffee essence and the sugar. Mix this with the chestnut purée and the softened butter. Shape it into a log. Leave the log in the fridge for a day to 'amalgamate'. Decorate with candied fruit or whipped cream. At Christmas we put fresh holly and chocolate shavings on it. We also put a few drops of some sort of drink in.

- It is better to go to the house of mourning, than to go to the house of feasting.

    Ecclesiastes, vii.1

Crème de Marron

Serves 6

1 large can sweetened marron purée

1–2 cups of cream (according to taste)
Lemon juice

Mix up a can of marron purée with whipped cream and a little lemon juice.

David Cheshire
Film Director's Delight

1 can sweet marron purée Sautéed almonds
Yoghourt

Fold enough yoghourt into the purée to suit your taste. Serve the mixture in glass bowls and cover it with sautéed almonds. The sweet and sour contrast is delicious. The sautéed almonds are essential for they create the impression that immense trouble has been taken.

Linda Kelly
Pineapple and Vanilla Cream

Pineapple (Libby's or fresh) Double cream
Vanilla ice cream

Serve slices of pineapple with sugar and a sauce made of melted vanilla ice cream (Cornish preferably) mixed with double cream. This tastes exactly like *crème vanille*, and has fooled everybody from ambassadors downward.

Cressida Connolly
Quince Joy

Serves 6

6 Petits Suisses   Quince jelly
$\frac{1}{4}$ pint double cream   Lemon juice

Mix all the ingredients together. The taste of the quince makes this dish unusual. The lemon juice is crucial for it helps bring out the flavour of the jelly.

186 *Darling, you shouldn't have gone to so much trouble*

- Young ladies should take care of themselves.
    Jane Austen (1775–1817)
    Emma

And what would you like for pudding?

Gooseberry Fool Ivana

1 can gooseberries   *Sugar*
Yoghourt   *Cream*

Blend all the ingredients and cool in the fridge. Serve in bowls and top with cream.

Francis Bacon
Syllabub

Serves 4

½ *pint thin cream*   *2 tablespoons caster sugar*
1 wine glass dry sherry   *Milk (optional)*
2 lemons

Squeeze the lemons and put the juice with all the ingredients into a large bowl. Whisk and skim the froth as it rises. Put froth into champagne glasses, continue whisking and skimming until all is used up. If cream gets too thick to produce froth, add a little milk.

Stand in ice box or refrigerator for 2 to 3 hours.

Old recipe
To Make a Syllabub Under the Cow

Put a bottle of strong beer and a pint of cyder into a punchbowl, grate in a small nutmeg, and sweeten it to your taste. Then milk as much milk from the cow as will make a strong froth, and the ale look clear, let it stand an hour, then strew over it a few currants, well washed, picked, and plumped before the fire, then send it to the table.

Cœur à la Crème

Serves 10

2 large packets Philadelphia cheese (softened if possible)	Sugar
	Lemon juice
2 large cartons whipping cream	Vanilla essence

Whip the cream stiff. Mash or blend the cream cheese. Mix together with some sugar, lemon juice and a dash of vanilla.

Pig's Pud

Serves 4

½ pint double cream
1 tablespoon lemon juice
Zest of 1 lemon, orange or tangerine

½ wine glass white wine
Sugar (caster) to taste

Beat the cream, being careful to stop short of turning it into butter. Carefully mix in the other ingredients. This is almost too rich to eat, so serve it after a rather *maigre* first course.

Strawberry Cream

Serves 6

1 lb strawberries (fresh, frozen or tinned)
½ pint cream
Sugar
Drop of kirsch

Whip the cream, fold in the chopped or blended strawberries with the kirsch and sugar to taste. Serve with *langue de chat* biscuits. This is one of the few dishes in which you can use tinned or frozen strawberries.

Another

1 lb cottage cheese (unsalted)
½ lb strawberries
4 tablespoons sugar

Liquidise strawberries and sugar. Add cottage cheese and liquidise until the mixture is a smooth cream.

Fay Maschler
Omelette Soufflé au Grand Marnier

Serves 2–3

Not exactly an original recipe but not many people seem to do it, and it is as easy as falling off your chair.

3 eggs
2 tablespoons caster sugar
A generous splash of Grand Marnier
A squeeze of lemon juice
Butter
Heated-up apricot jam or a cold purée of fresh soft fruit (optional)

Separate the eggs. Beat the yolks with the sugar, lemon juice and Grand Marnier. Beat the egg whites until they stand in snowy peaks. Heat a knob of butter in an omelette pan. Gently fold the whites into the yolk mixture. When the butter is foaming and just on the turn (to a nutty brown colour) pour in the mixture. It will set on the bottom and puff up slightly. Since the crust is the best bit, lift it and let a little more of the mixture hit the bottom of the pan. Do that once or twice again. Now fold the omelette over and serve. It is perfectly splendid like that but can be glorified with a sauce of apricot jam heated up and perhaps thinned with another glug of Grand Marnier, or a purée made from raspberries, blackberries, blackcurrants, etc., sweetened only marginally with sugar. These are best served cold as a contrast to the hot egg.

Henrietta Moraes
Thunder and Lightning
(traditional Cornish dish)

1 real honeycomb with wax   Cornish cream

Serve separately.

Obviously it's so rich it knocks people out – it makes them fly. You only need to eat a tiny bit. You eat the honey and the cream together on a spoon. The texture is so pure and sensual on the palate that I promise you it makes people swoon. I served it for lunch and my guests had been to a wedding the day before and they were so hung-over they were crawling. Thunder and Lightning revived them. You can't get ingredients purer than this.

- I can endure my own despair but not another's hope.
  William Walsh (1663–1708)
  Of All the Torments

Lemon Curd and Yoghourt Mousse

2–3 tablespoons lemon curd ¼ *pint double cream*
3 × 5 oz cartons natural yoghourt

Carefully stir yoghourt into lemon curd, whip cream and fold into yoghourt mixture.

Only syllabub is as easy to make, and this recipe is as imaginative and less well known. You can't spoil it by varying the proportions of the ingredients, but don't put them in a blender, or you will end up with a runny yoghourt soup.

You could also leave out the lemon curd and just sprinkle a lot of brown sugar over the yoghourt and cream mixture. Chill it well.

Orange Cheese

Serves 6

Take four oranges, 1 lb curd cheese, two tablespoons of single cream and sugar to taste. Peel two of the oranges, skin them and break into pieces. Squeeze the juice from the other two oranges, and put into blender with curd cheese, orange pieces, sugar and cream. Blend and chill. Serve in little glass dishes with slices of crystallised orange for decoration.

Junket

Serves 4

1 level tablespoon vanilla sugar	3 tablespoons rennet
1 pint milk	Nutmeg

You may have to hunt about for a shop that stocks rennet, as junket is rather out of favour today – which is absurd, since it is such a simple and pleasing dish.

Heat the milk (and sugar) until it is just lukewarm – dip the little finger of your left hand into the milk to test the temperature.* If it feels in the least uncomfortably hot, the junket will curdle. Add the rennet and pour into a shallow bowl. Grate a little nutmeg over it. Leave in a warm place until set, then chill. Serve covered with thick cream (unwhipped), decorated with damask rose, geranium, or clove pink petals.

Annie Freud
Oeufs à la Neige or Floating Islands

In France, I have never seen anyone beating egg whites by hand with a wire whisk in a copper bowl except at the famous restaurant Mère Poularde on the Mont Saint Michel, where incidentally, this work is done at the open window for the full benefit of the tourists. When I was passing in the street the whisking sound was so regular, rythmical and dominant over the other street activities that until I realised what it was, I

---

* If you are left-handed, use the little finger of your right hand, because the hand you use less often is always more sensitive than the other.

thought it must be some sort of local music or dance rhythm. Everyone else uses Moulinex.

Here is a spectacular and delicious sweet, not at all difficult to prepare.

Serves 4

1 pint milk
3 eggs
Pinch of salt
1 heaped tablespoon potato flour or arrowroot flour

5 oz caster sugar
Vanilla pod
Squeeze of lemon juice
1 tablespoon water

Place vanilla pod in milk, boil; allow to cool. Separate eggs, whip (using trusty machine) egg whites with pinch salt. Fold in sugar (1 oz).

Heat milk, drop scoops of stiff egg white on to milk and poach until firm, turning with perforated spoon (2 minutes). Remove egg whites and put on a plate.

Beat egg yolks with 3 oz sugar and flour. Add warm milk. Stir custard over low flame until slightly thickened. Pour custard into shallow dish, place meringue floats on it. Heat last ounce of sugar with water (1 tablespoon) and lemon juice until turning gold, let it trickle over peaks of 'islands'. Chill well before serving.

Margaret Reinhold, psychiatrist
Pots de Crème au Chocolat

Serves 6

1 × 6 oz packet choc chips
2 large eggs
2 tablespoons strong coffee
1 teaspoon rum or rum extract

1 teaspoon orange liqueur or apricot brandy
¾ cup scalded milk

Place chips, eggs, flavourings in blender and whirl 30 seconds; add hot scalded milk and whirl again. Pour into 6 *pot de crème* pots. Chill.

Margaret Reinhold
Applecake

Serves 6–8

1 pint cornflakes	A little butter
5 lb cooking apples	Cream
3 heaped teaspoons cinnamon	Grated chocolate
12 oz sugar	

Crush sugar, cinnamon and cornflakes. Grate apples (not cores). Squeeze water from grated apples. Put layers of cornflakes/sugar then apples, etc. in a round buttered cake tin. Double layer of cornflakes/sugar on top. Touch of butter on top. Cook for 45 minutes in a preheated oven, 375F (mark 5). When cooled, layer cream all over and grate chocolate lightly on top.

Cressida Connolly
Grape Crumble

Serves 4

1 can grapes	4 oz sugar
4 oz butter	4 oz flour

Make a crumble with the sugar, flour and butter. Place the grapes in a baking tin and cover them with the crumble. Bake until brown. When the canned grapes are baked they taste like fresh grapes and people think you have peeled and deseeded them.

Charlotte Bielenberg
Charlotte's Charlotte

Serves 6

1 packet bourbon biscuits
1½ lb apple purée (fresh or tinned)
1 packet lemon or lime jelly
Brown sugar

Make up the jelly with about ¾ pint of water. Line a bowl with the biscuits and trickle some of the jelly over to set them together. Mix the rest of the jelly with the apple and pour on to the biscuits. Chill. When thoroughly cold and set, sprinkle liberally with brown sugar. Put the bowl in a pan of iced water and slide under a red-hot grill until the sugar caramelises. Serve cold with whipped cream.

Neiti Gowrie
Cerises Ivres

Sponge finger biscuits (boudoir)
Hero black cherries
A little kirsch, brandy or whisky
Whipped cream

Dip the biscuits very quickly into brandy. Make layers of biscuits and cherries – without the juice – ending with a layer of cherries. Top with whipped cream. Make sure you use Hero's black cherries for this recipe and not the anaemic-looking kind that other brands produce.

Blackcurrant Flan

Buy a flan case. Into a boiling syrup of water and sugar (probably about ½ pint) put as many frozen blackcurrants as will fill the case. Cook only until the fruit has thawed. Add melted gelatine according to packet directions. Pour into the flan case and leave to set. Serve on a large plate decorated with geranium leaves.

Elizabeth Targett
Jamaican Crunch Pie

Serves 6

½ lb packet ginger nuts
¼ lb butter
¼ pint double cream

1 can sweetened condensed milk
 – about 7 oz size
6 tablespoons lemon juice
Grated rind of one lemon

Crush ginger nuts and place in bowl. Pour melted butter over them and mix evenly. Place mixture in 7½ inch platter to form smooth shell. Lightly whip the cream – fold in condensed milk, lemon juice and rind. When beginning to thicken, pour into biscuit shell. Chill in refrigerator overnight.

Patricia Radford,
Child psychoanalyst
Ginger Nut Dream

Serves 6

1 packet ginger nut biscuits
8 tablespoons sherry

Whipped double cream
Toasted almonds

Pour sherry into a saucer. Dip biscuits singly in sherry. Cover one side of biscuit thickly in cream. Form into log of alternate biscuits and cream. Spoon over remaining sherry and cream. Decorate with toasted almonds.

Patricia Radford
Zabaglione — quick

Family block vanilla ice cream   6 *tablespoons Marsala or other fortified wine*

Dig holes in ice cream – pour in spoonfuls of Marsala. Keep in freezer until required.

Remove from freezer at beginning of the meal. Serve in glasses with Pompadour wafers.

Strawberry Ice Cream

Serves 6

1 lb frozen or fresh strawberries, puréed
4 egg whites
8 oz caster sugar
½ pint double cream

Whisk the egg whites until they are stiff. Fold in the sugar, then the strawberry purée and lastly the whipped cream. Freeze. Serve in a pretty dish.

- Wife, into thy garden, and set me a plot,
  With strawberry roots, of the best to be got.

  Thomas Tusser (*c.* 1520–80)

Grapefruit Ice Cream

Serves 6

1 can (1 pint) grapefruit juice
2 egg yolks
1½ pints cream

Liquidise all ingredients in blender and freeze.

The richness of the cream and the tartness of the grapefruit juice combine beautifully.

New England Maple Pecan Ice Cream

Buy this ice cream in a shop and scoop it into a dish to look home-made. Serve maple syrup separately with it.

Loseley Farm ice cream can also be served without apology – as can many commercial water ices. Decorate with a little of the appropriate fruit – lemon slices, blackcurrants, etc. Orange water ice looks well strewn with marigold petals.

Most commercial ice creams taste as though they are composed of seal blubber and vanilla-flavoured whipped polystyrene, and are hard to disguise.

Theodora FitzGibbon
Store Cupboard Ice Cream

This has a surprisingly good flavour and is very easy to make.

1 small can evaporated milk *Sugar to taste (1–2 teaspoons)*
The above can full of milk *1 tablespoon coffee essence*
1 package Dream Topping *or any Jif topping (optional)*

Mix all ingredients and beat with a rotary or electric beater until thick and creamy, about 15 minutes by hand, but 2–3 minutes electrically. Do not overbeat as it could curdle. Put in a container and cover, then set in freezer part of fridge at normal setting for 12 hours. It can be flavoured with 1 tablespoon of coffee essence or any of the Jif toppings added to the milk, if a flavoured ice cream is wanted.

Honey Sundae

Vanilla ice cream *Chopped nuts*
Honey

Pour hot, melted honey over vanilla ice cream and sprinkle with chopped nuts.

**Angel Bacon,
Art Assistant, *Harpers & Queen* magazine**
Melting Mars Bars

Melt Mars Bars in bowl over hot water, add a dash of kirsch and pour over Cornish dairy ice cream. The effect is as of expensive fondue on freshly whipped ice cream!

Shelly Jerry

Serves 4

Measure a pint of water 1 wine glass short, and boil it. Make up a packet of lemon jelly and add 1 glass of sweet dark sherry. Set in fridge.

Alan Bennett
Bread and Butter and Cinnamon Pudding

Grease a deep basin. Lavishly butter as many slices of bread as you need to fill the dish. Sprinkle plenty of sultanas between each layer of bread.

Beat 2 eggs and 3 tablespoons of sugar together with a little milk. Add 1 small tin of evaporated milk plus a pint of ordinary milk, or as much as you need to fill the dish. Pour over the bread and leave to soak for half an hour.

Mix a cupful of breadcrumbs with 1 or 2 tablespoons of soft brown sugar and 2 teaspoons of cinnamon. Spread the mixture over the top of the pudding and cover with foil.

Cook at 275F (mark 1) for 1 hour. Remove the foil and cook at 300F (mark 2) for half an hour or until the pudding is risen and brown.

This can be served alone as a supper dish for tired children.

Alice Roosevelt Longworth,
from *The Cookbook of the Performing Artists of the Kennedy Center*

English Afternoon Tea

Mrs Longworth, the daughter of President Teddy Roosevelt, never cooked in her life, but her English afternoon teas were famous. Although she knew (and kept) many secrets, the only cookery 'secret' she knew, that of perfect bread and butter, she willingly imparted when asked to give her favourite recipe:

Take a loaf of very good unsliced bread; butter with sweet butter; cut a thin slice with a very sharp knife; repeat.

Coffee

> What pleases the palate nourishes.
> Hippocrates
>
> A little of what you fancy does you good.
> Common saying

Coffee is the most troublesome thing to produce after you have served a dinner. Instant coffee is disgusting, but Continental instant can be used if you make it in a tin pot. The taste of the tin helps to take away the taste of the 'instant'. Place *one* real coffee bean under the grill while you serve it. If a fantastic aroma of coffee pervades your dining room, guests can be deceived as to what they are drinking.

Turkish Coffee

This can be made at the table in a *rakweh* pot over a spirit flame. *Helwa* is very sweet, *Wasat* medium sweet, and *Sarda* has hardly any sugar.

Boil the water, add the sugar (1 teaspoon per person for *wasat*), remove *rakweh* from the flame and add finely ground dark coffee, the darkest you can get – lightly roasted, and mocha are too bitter – 1 teaspoon per person. Put *rakweh* back on the flame. Let it come to the boil 3 times.

You can flavour the coffee with cardamom seeds, which you add when you are boiling the water. You can also flavour each cupful with a few drops of orange blossom water. Dessert fruits and chocolates make this almost a course on its own.

Leonidas or Charbonnel et Walker or any other handmade chocolates are best.

Nicholas Haslam
Arabian Coffee

2 pints very strong Nescafé   Sugar to taste
2 tablespoons cocoa with a dash of vanilla

The thickness of the cocoa gives this coffee an aromatic and Arabian flavour.

Iced Coffee

The proper way to do this is to add to 1 part strong black coffee (chilled) 2 parts chilled milk. Sweeten lightly with icing sugar. The easy way is to use Camp coffee instead. Add to taste to cold milk. In both cases add ice cubes.

Jasmine Tea

Infuse the leaves briefly, then pour the tea into another warmed pot. More refreshing than coffee after a heavy meal.

Food for Children

> I thank the goodness and the grace
> Which on my birth have smiled,
> And made me, in these Christian days,
> A happy English child.
>
> Jane Taylor (1783–1824)
> *A Child's Hymn of Praise*

While children should obviously eat as much pure, fresh food as possible, unfortunately their inclinations seem to lie in the opposite direction.

Spotty teenagers and teething toddlers alike find lettuce and plain unsweetened yoghourt depressing, and prefer hamburgers and chips and chocolate cake. They will learn better in time if you usually give them proper food, but it will do them little harm if occasionally, when worn out by the strife, you offer them the unwholesome but satisfying dishes they crave.

The following dishes are of the buccaneering type they would not be ashamed to see produced when their friends come round.

Sandwiches

Toasted sandwiches always appear more substantial than the ordinary sort and make a good light supper for a child, provided you use wholemeal bread and also supply some raw fruit or salad. Grated cheese, pounded cooked chicken, or meat, chopped hard-boiled egg are all suitable fillings.

- Q: Why is it impossible to starve in the desert?
  A: Because of all the sand which is there.

Soda Bread
(useful for breadless emergencies)

1 lb plain flour
½ oz baking powder
1 teaspoon salt
Sour milk to mix (about ¼ pint)

Sieve dry ingredients together. Make a well and pour in the milk – if you have no sour milk, use yoghourt thinned with fresh milk. Mix together for as short a time as possible and form into a ball. Flatten this on a floured surface until it is a circle about 1 inch thick. Cut it into quarters and cook it on top of the stove on a preheated griddle iron for 20 minutes – 10 each side. A cast iron frying pan will do.

Soups

For a late supper for children there is nothing more nourishing than a vegetable soup with toasted brown bread. Use up cooked vegetables – blended with milk or stock. Small quantities of fresh vegetables also cook very quickly. Use a small amount of water and blend all together.

Margaret Powell
Fish Surprise

Serves 4

1 packet potato powder – the enough-for-three size	Breadcrumbs
1 packet parsley sauce	Dash of anchovy sauce
1 × 7 oz can salmon	Butter

Reconstitute the potato powder, adding a knob of butter and, if any, a teaspoon of cream. Put into a fire-proof dish, leaving a hole in the centre. Tip the salmon into the hole, adding the dash of anchovy sauce. Reconstitute the parsley sauce and pour over the salmon. Sprinkle with the breadcrumbs. Dot with small pieces of butter and heat in the oven for 20 minutes, 350–375F (mark 4–5). If not brown on top by then, place under hot grill for a few minutes.

Tuna Casserole

Serves 4–6

1 can condensed chicken or mushroom soup	1 can tuna fish
2 cans cream-style corn	1 chopped green pepper
	Finely chopped onion

Mix up all ingredients in a buttered casserole dish and bake in a very hot oven for 15 minutes.

Children love this casserole as it looks colourful and contains all their favourite foods. It is also so nourishing that you don't have to feel guilty about giving them toasted cheese sandwiches for the next meal.

Oliver's Pizza

Greek pitta bread (flat unleavened bread)
Tomato purée
Anchovies, onions, halved olives, sliced mushrooms, grated cheese or anything you would put on a pizza

Split the pitta bread in half and toast it on the outside. Spread the tomato purée on the inside of the bread, cover it with anchovies, etc. and put it under the grill.

Boiled Rice Delight

Any frozen, tinned or left-over vegetables, e.g., peas, beans, diced carrots
Small can sweetcorn
Frankfurters or Viennas or cooked diced chicken
Boiled rice
Soy sauce (optional)

Mix rice with vegetables. Put in steamer with sliced sausage on top. Steam for ten to fifteen minutes. If you substitute cooked diced chicken for the sausage and add soy sauce at the end you can tell them they are having a Chinese meal.

Roald Dahl
Norwegian Cauliflower

Serves 4–6

1 cauliflower   Béchamel sauce
1 bag of frozen prawns or shrimps

Make a béchamel sauce. Add the defrosted prawns. Pour this mixture over the cooked cauliflower. A traditional Norwegian dish, easy to make and delicious. A great supper for children.

Connie Strigner
Hamburgers

Get your butcher to put chuck steak once through the mincer and you can make hamburgers that would put every take-away in the country out of business. Put the minced meat in a bowl, stir in chopped onion and a raw egg, add parsley, salt, pepper and a squeeze of garlic if you like it. Shape the mixture into patty cakes and fry in hot oil until brown. They really are good and make a bought hamburger taste like cattle food.

Connie Strigner
Mixed Grill

Mixed grills are more expensive but they take very little time to cook. They can consist of any combination of chops, steak, kidneys, bacon, sausages, and eggs, and to make up for the cost of the meats you can serve them with cheap but delicious bubble and squeak. This is a mixture of cold potato and cold greens fried together until they have a crisp, nutty, brown underblanket. I had it once in a famous restaurant and they charged the earth. I cook it better too.

- What is patriotism but the love of good things we ate in our childhood.

Lin Yutang (b. 1895)

Curried Spam

Serves 6

1 can Spam	Curry powder
1 can tomatoes	1 tablespoon oil
Chopped onion	Sultanas

Dice the Spam. Lightly fry the onion in the oil and add the Spam. Turn and stir a bit, add the curry powder and then the tomatoes and sultanas. Cook until the liquid has reduced slightly and the sultanas plumped up. Do not add salt – Spam is salty already. Serve with rice.

Chilli Con Carne

Serves 6

1 lb mince	Oil and tabasco
1 small can baked beans	1 clove of garlic
2 cups frozen mixed vegetables	or small chopped onion
1 tablespoon tomato purée	

Lightly fry the mince and onion or garlic, add the other ingredients and a very little water. Add as much or as little tabasco as the children will stomach – children's tolerance of hot dishes varies greatly but they all like the idea of this dish.

If you substitute tinned kidney beans for the baked beans this can be offered to adults.

Baked Chicken

Pieces of chicken
Bottled Italian salad dressing
Seasoned breadcrumbs

Marinate the pieces of chicken in bottled Italian salad dressing. Then roll them in seasoned breadcrumbs and bake them in the oven for 1 hour. This tastes like take-away chicken and therefore children find it more acceptable than *coq au vin*.

Frank Stapleton's Cheese Pudding

Feeds one professional footballer, or three to four little ones

4 eggs
Breakfastcupful of fresh white breadcrumbs
4 oz grated Cheddar cheese
1 oz butter
Salt, pepper, mustard

Beat eggs, add seasoning. Melt butter, pour in eggs and cook until beginning to thicken. Add breadcrumbs and cheese and cook until absorbed, stirring all the time.

or

Combine all the ingredients. Leave until required. Cook in medium oven, 375F (mark 5) until risen and golden brown.

Potato Scones

1 small packet instant potato
½ pint milk
4 oz self-raising flour
2 oz melted butter or margarine
Pinch of salt

Make up the potato with the boiling milk and add the melted butter or margarine. Mix in the flour. Turn on to a floured baking tray. Mould and flatten to a rough circle. Score segments on top. Cook in hot oven for 15–20 minutes. Eat hot, with butter. Flattened more, it can be used as a pizza base.

Foolproof Scones

1 lb self-raising flour
½ teacup oil
½ teacup milk
1 dessertspoon sugar
Pinch of salt
Dried fruit (optional)

To the bowl of flour, sugar and salt, add the oil and milk, which you have poured into the same teacup. Mix. Add more milk if the mixture is too dry, or flour if the mixture seems too runny. Put spoonfuls on a greased baking sheet and bake in a hot oven for 10–15 minutes. If you leave out the sugar and fruit and add grated cheese you have cheese scones. Sprinkle the top of each with a few shreds of the grated cheese.

Fruit Cake

¼ pint water
4 oz margarine
4 oz sugar (brown or
　　white and brown mixed)
6 oz fruit
1 beaten egg
8 oz self-raising flour
½ teaspoon mixed spice

Boil first 4 ingredients gently for 20 minutes and cool slightly. Mix the beaten egg, self-raising flour and mixed spice into the above mixture. Pour into greased baking tin and sprinkle brown sugar on top. Cook at 350F (mark 4) for about 45 minutes.

Flapjacks

3 oz margarine　　4 oz oats
3 oz sugar

Melt margarine, mix in sugar and oats. Press into well greased shallow dish. Cook at the top of oven 350F (mark 4) for about 20 minutes. Allow to cool slightly before slicing and lift out of dish when just warm.

Krispy Kisses

Melt together in a large bowl over a pan of boiling water a bar each of milk and plain chocolate. When they are quite melted pour in as many rice crispies or cornflakes as the mixture will hold. Drop teaspoonfuls on to paper cases on baking sheet and leave to set.

Banana Cheesecake

1 banana　　1 packet instant cheesecake mix

Make up the base according to packet directions. Mash the

banana and mix well with the prepared filling. Chill before serving.

Coconut Haystacks

8 oz dessicated coconut
Few drops vanilla essence
2 oz sugar
1 egg

Mix all together, press spoonfuls of the mixture into an eggcup and bang down smartly on to a greased baking sheet. Cook 8–10 minutes in a moderate oven.

Ivana Citkovitz
Ivana's Pudding

Peanut butter   Sharwood's chocolate sauce

Put some (unsalted) peanut butter in ice cream dishes and cover it with chocolate sauce.

Toby's Pudding

Take 1 tin of condensed milk. Do not open it. Place it in a pan and half cover with water. Boil for 3–4 hours in tin, making sure water remains at same level. Allow to cool. Open tin and – *olé* – a disgustingly sweet brown pudding.

Palmiers

1 packet frozen puff pastry   Granulated sugar

Roll pastry out in the sugar. Fold sides to the middle and then in half. Cut in $\frac{1}{4}$ inch slices. Sprinkle with sugar again. Place in greased baking tray, not too close together. Cook for 10 minutes in a hot oven.

Can be sandwiched together with cream or topped with cream and fresh strawberries or raspberries.

Upside-Down Cake

Packet of cake mixture *Canned pineapple*

Follow directions on the package and pour the cake mixture into a baking tin in which you have first placed the pineapple slices. After your cake is baked, turn the tin upside down so the pineapple will come out on top and be a pretty and tasty decoration.

Theodora FitzGibbon
Lemon Curd Spread

This can be made in minutes, and if left for 2 hours to thicken makes a good, original spread for bread and butter or as a cake filling. Beat together 1 small can condensed milk with the finely grated rind and juice of 1 lemon and 1 egg yolk. Orange can also be used.

Cake Filling

8 oz sugar *1 or 2 teaspoons of fruit squash*
1 oz unsalted butter

Combine in a blender or food processor.

Instant Lemonade

2 lemons *Water*
Sugar to taste *Sprig of mint (optional)*
A few ice cubes

Put the sugar, lemons, ice and mint and enough water to cover the blades in the blender or food processor. Blend until the lemons are well minced, pour through sieve into a wide-mouthed jug and add sufficient soda water or water to dilute.

Banana Milk Shake

2 bananas   *1 pint milk*
Sugar to taste   *Ice*

Blend bananas, sugar, ice and enough milk to cover blades. Add remainder of milk. You can substitute strawberries or raspberries for the bananas.

- Women can spin very well; but they cannot make a good book of cookery.
  Dr Johnson (1709–1784)

- You ought certainly to forgive them as a Christian.
  Jane Austen (1775–1817)
  Pride and Prejudice

Index

Aigrettes, Instant, 71
Alexander, 50
Allen, Myrtle, 81, 115
Almond Soup, 80
Anchovy: butter, 156; Eggs, 66; Roll, 60; Sauce, 155–6
Antipasto, 70
Aperitifs, 48–9
Applecake, 193
Aronson, Zara Baar: *quoted*, 12
Attic Cutlets, 124
Austen, Jane: *quoted*, 51, 186, 217
Avocado: Bacon & Lettuce Salad, 70; Baked, 70; Caroline, 69; Chez Solange, 69; Prawn Soup, 79

Baba Ghanouch, 169
Bacon, Angel, 198
Bacon, Francis, 151, 186; *quoted*, 152, 179
Bacon Recipe, Travelling, 147
Baekland, Elizabeth, 57, 88
Bainbridge, Beryl, 142
Balzac, Honoré de: *quoted*, 138
Banana: Cheesecake, 214; Cream, 183; Daiquiri, 51; Dessert, 183; Milk Shake, 217
Barbecue Sauce, 154
Baro, Gene, 128
Bean: Green, Salad, 171; Salad, 175
Beef: & Bacon Loaf, 144; Cold, 116; Cubes, 115–16
Beeton, Mrs: *quoted*, 12
Bennett, Alan, 198
Bielenberg, Charlotte, 165, 194
Bisque, Quick, 77
Black Velvet, 46
Blackcurrant Flan, 194–5
blenders, 33–4
Blinis, 58
Boeuf Gentleman, 117
Bootes-Johns, Louise, 100
Borscht, 85
Boud, Janet, 101
Brandy Butter, 157

bread, 22–3, 207–8
Bread & Butter & Cinnamon Pudding, 198
Breech, Jean, 121, 129
Brigstocke, Heather, 179
Brussels Sprout Soup, 81
Bull Shot, 49
Burgul Salad, 170
butter, 23
butters, 156–7
Byrne, Eileen, 64

Cabbage: Red, & Frankfurters, 165–6; Stir-Fried, 165
cakes, 22, 213–14; Filling, 216
Calder, Liz, 170
can opener, wall, 31
Carrot & Garlic Salad, 174
Cartland, Barbara, 97, 98
Casserole, Vegetable, 161
Cauliflower: Norwegian, 210; & Tomato Salad, 170
Caviar, 57; Soup, 90; Spaghetti, 141
Cerises Ivres, 194
Champagne: Cocktail, 46; Cup, 51–2; Frambois, 46
Charlotte's Charlotte, 194
cheese, 24; Fetta, 72; & Onion Soufflé, 146; Pudding, Frank Stapleton's, 212
Cheshire, David, 182, 185
Chicken: American & Pineapple Salad, 134; Baked, 212; Breasts, Uncle Gene's, 128; Cream, 127 Egyptian, 129; in Pâté Sauce, 132; Liver Marsala, 129; Liver Pâté, Magimix, 65; One-Dish, 132; Potted, 66; & Salami, 133; Soup, 88–9; Spicy, 126–7; Tandoori, 128
Chicory & Egg Salad, 67–8
children, food for, 205–17
Chilli Con Carne, 211–12
Citkovitz, Ivana, 215

Claret Cup, 52
cocktails, 36, 39–54
Coconut Haystacks, 215
Cod's Roe Pâté, 61
Cœur à la Crème, 187
coffee, 201–4; machine, 34
Colcord, Ann, 141
Coles, Gladys Mary, 147
Coleslaw, 173
Colin's Killer, 46
Connolly, Cressida, 185, 193
Cook, Boiled, 125
cookers: Aga, 33; infra-red, 33; microwave, 33; pressure, 32; slow, 32
cook's measure, 31
Coolers, 44
Cooper, Vanna, 155
Coquilles des Fruits de Mer Parisiennes, 95–6
Cordero La Chilindron, 123
Courgettes Farcies Avgolemono, 136–7
Cowan, Rex, 90, 109
Crab: with Ginger & Spring Onion, 107; Soup, 78–9
Crabmeat à la King, 97
cream, 23
Crème de Marron, 184
Crisp, Quentin, 92
croûtons, 77
Crudités, 71
Cucumber: Salad, 174; Soup, Cold, 86; Soup with Dill, Hot, 85
Curry: Mushroom & Nuts, 164; Spam, 211; Vegetable, 162
Curtis, Denis, 123

Dahl, Roald, 210
Daiquiri, 42
Daniel, Professor Glyn, 59
Date & Nut Salad, 170
Davenport, Philippa, 87
Deffand, Madame du: *quoted*, 15
Denman, Cara, 102, 181
Descartes, René: *quoted*, 29
Detmolderhof Cocktail, 59
Dickens, Charles: *quoted*, 173
Drinker's Sunday Lunch, 120
Dubonnet, 48
duck, 134–5; Sauce for, 154

Dunn, Ann, 71, 80, 144, 166, 167

Ecclesiastes: *quoted*, 184
Eels, Jellied, 62–3
Egg Sour, 55
Eggs: & Shrimps, Scrambled, 59–60; Smashed, 147; Ukrainian, 146

Faithfull, Marianne, 119
Fennel, Baked, 166
Field, Eugene: *quoted*, 132
Filets de Sole Caprice, 98
Film Director's Delight, 185
first courses, 55–73
fish, 17, 18, 93–109; Fast, 104–5; Florentine, 101; for children, 208–9; in a Dish, 104; Pie, Quick, 108; Sauce for, 153; Soup, Korean, 78; Soup, Quick, 80; Stanley's, 107; Steaks with Aïoli, 106; Surprise, 208
FitzGibbon, Theodora, 143, 145, 197, 216
Fizzes, 43–4
Flapjacks, 214
Fleischmann, Suzy, 130
Flips, 50
Floating Islands, 191–2
Foges, Gully, 141
food, presentation of, 36–7
food processors, 33–4
Fraser, Lady Antonia, 183
French '76, 45
Freud, Annie, 191
Freud, Lucian, 81
fruit 21; Cake, 214; Salad, Once-a-Year, 182

gadgets, kitchen, 30–4
garlic: butter, 156; press, 31
Gazpacho, Stanley's, 88
Gentleman, Sue, 117
Ginger Nut Dream, 195
Gooseberry Fool Ivana, 186
Gordon, Jane Conway, 72, 116
Gordon, Nigel, 97, 98
Gordon, Noële, 59
Goulash, Slapdash, 130
Gowrie, Neiti, 194
Gowrie's Fowl, Earl of, 125–6

Grandma's Dish, 168
Granville, Countess of, 90
Grape: Crumble, 193; Salad, 182
Grapefruit: Ice Cream, 196; Noilly Prat Sorbet, 109–10
graters, 31
Green butter, 157
Gregory, Professor Richard, 148*n*
Gross, Miriam, 119
Grossmith, George & Weedon: *quoted*, 122

Haddock, Captain's, 101; *see also* Kedgeree
Ham Stroganoff, 116
Hamburgers, 210
Hardie, Xandra, 80
Haslam, Nicholas, 77, 152, 203
Haynes, Victor, 132
Heaney, Mrs Seamus, 61
herbs, 25; chopping, 31
Herring, Soused, 102
Highballs, 48–9
Hippocrates: *quoted*, 203
Hogg, Minn, 147
Hollandaise: Fake, 152; Quick, 153
Honey Sundae, 197–8
Horseradish, Mock, 154
Hotpot, Quicker Better, 125
Housman, A. E.: *quoted*, 121
Howell, Georgina, 139
Hummus, 168

Ice Cream, 185, 196–7; Parmesan Cheese, 73; Tomato, 72–3
Indian Domestic Economy & Cookery: quoted, 113
ingredients, 15–29
Isaiah: *quoted*, 161
Ivana's Pudding, 215

Jamaican Crunch Pie, 195
jams, 28
Japanese Quick Soup, 78
Jazzar, Mouna, 121, 168, 169
jellies, 28
Johnson, Dr: *quoted*, 181, 217
Jones, Helen, 114, 153
Joyce, T. Athol, 140
Juleps: Champagne, 45; Mint, 45

Junket, 191

Kahn, Toni Harrison, 70, 105
Kedgeree, 99–100; Hungry Horse, 99
Kelly, Linda, 185
Kende, Rosa, 118
Kennedy, William, 128, 144
Kidneys in their Jackets, 139
Kippers, 58
Kir Genia, 53
Kiwi Fruit Ice, 179
knives, 31
Kobayashi, Kuniko, 78
Krispy Kisses, 214

Lamb: Cutlets in Fresh Lemon Juice, 124; Stuffed with Anchovies, 121; Syrian, Leg of, 121–2
Landels, Willie, 66
La Pêche de Bacchus, 179–80
Lawley, Sue, 126
Lefcowitz, Mary, 173
Left-overs, 28–9
Lemon Curd: Spread, 216; & Yoghourt Mousse, 190
Lemonade, Instant, 216–17
Lentil: Soup, Quick Thick, 82–3; Stew *Hausfrauenart*, Brown, 167–8
Lincoln, Abraham: *quoted*, 41
Lisle, Vanessa de, 73
Liver, Chopped, 130–1
Lloyd, Julian, 101
Lobster Salad, 103
Lokchen Soup, 90–1
Longworth, Alice Roosevelt, 199
'Lucrezia', 84
Luigi, 42

MacGregor, Sue, 88
Mackerel: Classic, 105; Smoked, Pâté, 61
main courses, 111–48, 208–12
Maltaise, Fake, 152
mandoline, 31
Mardi Gras, 42
margarine, 23
Markham: *quoted*, 133
Marks, Ailish, 104

Mars Bars, Melting, 198
Martinis, 48
Maschler, Fay, 63, 107, 139, 155, 163, 188
May Dinner, 137
Mayonnaise, 26–7; Fake, for Masking Cold Chicken, 152; Thick, Fat, Genuine, 151–2
measurements (*table*), 35
meat, 16–18, 28–9, 113–44, 147–8, 210–12
Melon: Framboise, 181; & Parma Ham, 72
Meredith, George: *quoted*, 67, 189
Merwyn, Dido, 145
milk, 23
Miller, Rachel & Jonathan, 172
Mint Jelly, 153
Mixed Grill, 210–11
mixers, 33–4
Mlinaric, David, 66
Moore, Sue Parkin, 89
Moraes, Henrietta, 189
Moss, Stanley, 107
Mott, George, 166
mousse, 64–5, 190
Mulhern, Zita, 65, 164
Mushrooms: à la Grecque, 172; & Nuts, Curried, 164
mustard, 26

Nasturtium Salad, 170
New Century Cookery Book, The: *quoted*, 57
New England Maple Pecan Ice Cream, 197

O'Casey, Brenda, 108
Oeufs: à la Neige or Floating Islands, 191–2; en Geleé, 67
oils, 24–5
Omelette: Cold, 144; Dido's, 145; Soufflé au Grand Marnier, 188–9
Onions: Baked, 166; Sauce, 153
Orange: Cheese, 190–1; & Onion Salad, 174
Orwell, Sonia, 118, 140
Oysters, 57

Palmiers, 215

Parsnips, Spiced, 163–4
Pasta, 18–19; with Bacon & Mushrooms, 141; Gritty, 139; *see also* spaghetti; tagliatelli
pastry, 22
pâté, 61, 65
Pea Soup, Cheat's, 88
Peaches & Raspberries, 180
Pears, Popote Stilton, 71
Peasants' Salad, 172
Pêches au Champagne, 179–80
Pepper Dip, 169
Peter, Chef, Popote Restaurant, 71
Pig's Pud, 187–8
Pineapple & Vanilla Cream, 185
Piperade, Variation on, 167
Pizza, Oliver's, 209
Poe, Edgar Allan: *quoted*, 63
Poet's Pie, 147–8
Pollo alla Cacciatore, 133–4
Pope, Alexander: *quoted*, 77, 184
Pork: Chops with Ginger in Orange Juice, 118–19; Chops with Smash, 118; Different Sweet/Sour, 119; Fillet of, in Cream, 119; Fillet of, in Wine Sauce, 118
Potato(es): in their Jerseys, 162; Salad, Hot, 165; Scones, 212; Soup, 82; Waistcoat, 162; *see also* Torta di Patate
pots, cooking, 32
Pots de Crème au Chocolat, 192–3
Powell, Margaret, 208
Prawn(s): Butter, 156; Willie's, 100–1
puddings, 177–99, 215–16
Punch, Oxford, 53
Pyke, Magnus, 100

Quatre, Henri: *quoted*, 126
Queen's Shape, 66–7
Quince Joy, 185

Rabbit, Blanket of, 136
Radford, Patricia, 195, 196
Raspberry Ice & Fire, 180
Ratatouille, 161–2
Reinhold, Margaret, 192, 193
relishes, 26
Restaurants: Ballymaloe, 81, 115;

Index   223

Bertorelli Bros., 89, 133; Castletown, 104; Drones, 79; Hungry Horse, 99; Neal Street, 70; Popote, 71; Ritz, 95, 179; White Tower, 136
Rhubarb, Stewed, 182
Rice, 18; Delight, Boiled, 209–10
Rimbaud, Arthur: *quoted*, 59
Rippon, Angela, 104
Rochon, Mrs T., 69
Rognons à L'Epicure, 138
Ross, Jennifer, 153
Rowlands, Eluned, 109
Rum: Banana, 183; Hot Buttered, 54; Toddy, 54
Ruskin, John: *quoted*, 58
Russian Salad, 175
Ryan, Mrs Richard, 78, 154

Sabayon, 97
Salade Niçoise, 174–5
salads, 29, 67, 70–1, 103, 165, 166, 170–5; Once-a-Year Fruit, 182; spinner, 31
Salis, Mrs de: *quoted*, 15
Salmon: Bread Soufflé, 102–3; Cold, 105; Mousse, 64; Steaks Baked in Silver Foil, 104
Salsa Verde, 153
sandwiches, 207
Sangria, 52–3
sardines, 62, 100
Saturday Salad, 172
sauces, 26–7, 149–57
Sauternes Cup, 52
Savarin, Brillat-: *quoted*, 103, 130
Schulenburg, Sheila, 120
Scilly Soup, 109
Scones, Foolproof, 213
Shakespeare, William: *quoted*, 119, 143, 146, 151
Shaw, Bernard, salads, 170
Shelley, Percy Bysshe: *quoted*, 15
Shelly Jerry, 198
Shrimps: in Cream & Dill, 103; Sautéed with Garlic, 63
Soda Bread, 207–8
Solomon, Song of: *quoted*, 98
sorbet, 109–10

soufflés, 102, 145, 146
Soupe Mauvaise Femme, 84
soups, 16, 75–92, 208
Spam, Curried, 211
Spaghetti: Carbonara, 140; Caviar, 141; Vanna's Italian Sauce for, 155
Spender, Natasha, 146
spices, 25–6
Spinach & Bacon Salad, 166–7
spoons, measuring, 30
Stacpoole, H. De Vere: *quoted*, 37
Steak(s): à la Huancaina, 114; Hot Cold, 113; Japanese, 113; Tartare, 114–15
Stew, Quick Green, 117
stews, 117, 167–8
stock, 27
Store Cupboard Ice Cream, 197
Stovies, 142–3
Stracciatella Soup, 89
Straughton, Bill, 99
Strawberry: Cream, 188; Ice Cream, 196
Strigner, Connie, 83, 210
Stuart, Lady, 182
stuffings, 28
sugar, 25*n*
Summer: Dish, 57; Soup, 89
syllabub, 186–7

Tagliatelli with Truffles, 140
Targett, Elizabeth, 195
Taylor, Jane: *quoted*, 207
Tea: English Afternoon, 199; Jasmin, 204
Tequila Sunrise, 41–2
Thomas, N. W., 140
Thorne, Patricia, 130
Thunder & Lightning, 189
timing device, automatic, 32
toasters, automatic, 34
Toby's Pudding, 215
Tomato: Ice Cream, 72–3; Salad, 171; Soup au Naturel, 81; Soup with Basil, Iced, 87; Soup with Dill, 87
Tongue Schadenfreude, 137–8
Torta di Patate, 143–4
tray, hot, 34

224 Index

Trout with Lemon & Butter, Fresh, 106
Tuna: Casserole, 209; Pâté, 61
Tunney, Kieran, 82
Turkey, Legless, 135
Tusser, Thomas: *quoted*, 196
Twain, Mark: *quoted*, 77

Upside-Down Cake, 216

Veg, Quicker Than Quick, 164
vegetables, 19–20, 159–75, 210
Vermouth Aperitif, 49
Vigny, Alfred de: *quoted*, 96, 125
Viney, M. Jacques, 95, 179
Virgil: *quoted*, 16, 105, 148
Vitello Tonnato, 120

Walsh, William: *quoted*, 189
Ward, Rev. Nathaniel: *quoted*, 45

Ward 9, 42
Watercress Soup, 84
Webster, John: *quoted*, 137
Whisky Toddy, 54
Whitehead, Alfred North: *quoted*, 138
Williams, Ursula Vaughan, 61, 83
wok, 32, 165
Wollheim, Day & Richard, 184
Worde, Wynkyn de: *quoted*, 126
Workhouse Soup, Tibetan, 92

yoghourt, 23; Lemon Curd &, Mousse, 190; Mousse, 65
Yule Log, 184
Yutang, Lin: *quoted*, 211
Yvonne's Washing-day Soup, 83

Zabaglione, Quick, 196